Cartomancy in Folk Witchcraft: Playing Cards and Marseille Tarot in Divination, Magic, & Lore

Copyright © 2019, 2022 by Roger J. Horne. All rights reserved. Second Edition.

No part of this book may be used or reproduced in any manner whatsoever without the prior written permission of the copyright holder.

ISBN 978-1-7367625-2-3
Moon over the Mountain Press

Cartomancy in Folk Witchcraft:
Playing Cards and Marseille Tarot in Divination, Magic, & Lore

Expanded Second Edition

Roger J. Horne

Contents

Introduction..7
Understanding the Cards...13
Reflecting on the Marseille Trumps....................115
Reading the Cards...135
Conjuring the Cards..155
Addendum: Games of Fortuna............................197

Introduction

The book you now hold in your hands is inspired by the tradition of literature from the mid-1800s detailing cartomantic operations, including works such as *Mother Bunch's Golden Fortune-Teller* (1857), *The New Fortune Book or Conjurer's Guide* (1850), and *The Spaewife or Universal Fortune-Teller* (1827). In the age of these concise books, now long passed, the reader could explore a variety of cartomantic methods and rhyming mnemonics without spending a fortune. Their methods were simple and accessible to all, designed for use by common folk. Anyone could pick up a deck of cards and begin to explore the subtle arts of cartomancy. In the spirit of this tradition, this work is intended to be both clear and practical.

Today, one can find any number of oracle decks in a variety of themes and art styles, so why should the modern witch bother to train in the discipline of old folk cartomancy? Put simply, folk cartomancy offers us a connection to our past and to arts that are skill-based rather than product-based, cunning rather than consumerist. By learning these methods and approaches, the witch can read with cards in a variety of styles, including the elusive tarot minors in unillustrated decks like the Marseille tarot. The history of folk cartomancy is old and rich indeed.

In fact, evidence suggests the existence of diverse folk-magical practices involving cards long before the modern tarot systems we know today, which are largely influenced by 20th century occultists like Arthur Edward Waite and Aleister Crowley. Huson (2004) notes that *La Spagna Istoriata*, published in 1519, makes reference to making a circle and "throwing the cards." Pierre de l'Ancre (1622) notes the use of cards to forge pacts with devils. In *Witchcraft and the Inquisition in Venice, 1550-1650*, Martin (1989) describes alleged witches Angela and Isabella Bellochio, who supposedly used cards extensively in their rites. Leland's (1899) collection of Italian folklore published as *Aradia:*

The Gospel of the Witches of Italy lists the ability to "divine by cards" as a gift given to those who follow the path of witchcraft. Unfortunately, the practitioners who belonged to these currents of cartomancy were not so fortunate as to bequeath their work in the form of a cohesive tradition. Instead, it is up to us to reconstruct their wisdom from the fragments we collect like jewels.

In the spirit of the lore in this tradition, this book makes unapologetic reference to those dark spirits and powers associated with witches in centuries past. This is common stuff in folkloric and traditional currents of the craft, and the seemingly diabolical elements of this volume's practices should be interpreted through the lens of the folkloric Devil rather than the biblical one, for these figures are, in fact, quite distinct. A more complete discussion of these underpinnings and their importance is provided in my previous work, *Folk Witchcraft: A Guide to Lore, Land, and the Familiar Spirit for the Solitary Practitioner*. In any case, in my personal practice, I have found that so-called "dark" entities are often misunderstood and can be kind and powerful allies when approached with good manners and common sense. These two principles are, in fact, good advice for most things related to witchcraft.

This little book, reader, is a love letter to the folk-cartomantic literature tradition, to the art of playing cards and Marseille tarot cards themselves, and to the pursuit of the deep wisdom in those images that have been called "the Devil's picture-book." May the doors to that wisdom be ever open to you. May you find inspiration for your own practice in these pages.

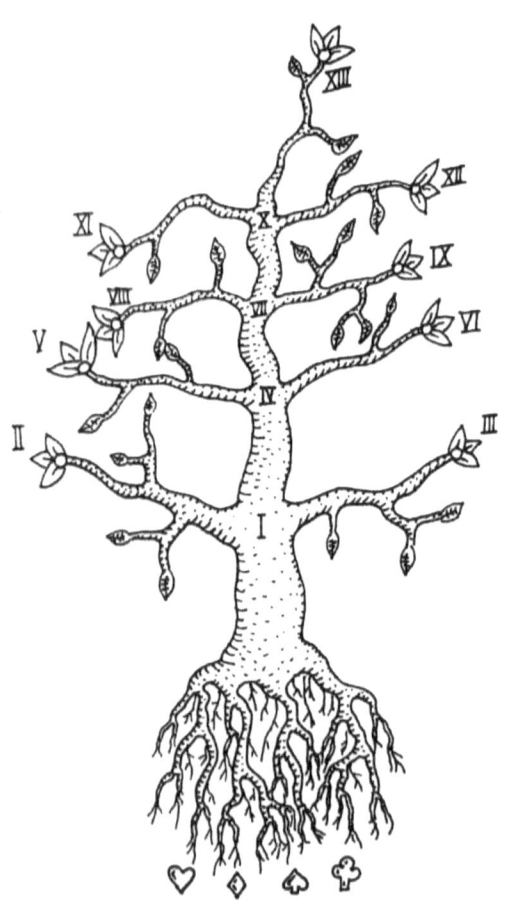

Understanding the Cards

The first lines of the following rhyme introduce the deck of playing cards as a book authored by the Devil himself. According to Nigel Jackson (2016), it was John Northbrooke in 1519 who described cards used to play games as "an invention of the Deuill." One wonders whether Northbrooke did the Devil injury or service, though, since the association of Old Nick with games and cards only further emphasized his free and fun-loving nature in folklore. Our opening rhyme is written in this spirit, and in the spirit of the numerous rhyming mnemonic devices of folk-divinatory traditions.

The Devil's Picture-Book:
A Cartomantic Mnemonic

Fifty-two the pages count
in the Devil's picture-book:
thirteen signs within four suits
of blood, knife, stone, and crook.

Blood to cherish loved ones;
a knife to joys divide;
stone to keep all treasures;
a crook to firmly guide.

Ace to start the journey,
and two to make a pair;
three, a sapling growing,
and four, a stable chair.

Five to throw the carriage,
and six to gather grain;
seven spelling wickedness,
and eight to take the reins.

Nine, a cornucopia,
and ten, completion's crown;

A joker in the book makes jest
at Fate's wheel spinning round.

Jacks are ever-learning,
and queens are ever-wise.
Kings seek to gain power,
by force and might to rise.

Although the aces, twos, threes, and fours are similar in nature here to Dawn Jackson's (n.d.) attributions in her fine poem, "For the Witch of Poor Memory," which has introduced so many witches to the arts of cartomancy, my own approach differs on most points based on my own preferences and experiences as a reader.

The common deck of playing cards includes twelve court or "face" cards (jacks, queens, and kings), numbered cards from one to ten in four suits, and (sometimes) jokers. If we do not count the jokers due to their unique nature in the deck, that leaves a total of thirteen cards in each suit, the number of moons in a year and a special sign associated with the work of witches. In the witch-lore collected by Davis (1975) in his volume titled *The Silver Bullet*, American witches were said to gather on Friday the thirteenth to work charms and craft special tools.

Having evolved from the same source as our modern deck of playing cards, the Marseille Tarot is similar in structure, being composed again of four suits: cups, swords, rods, and coins. These are simply alternate variations of the hearts, spades, clubs, and diamonds seen in the playing card suits. Unlike modern iterations of tarot that utilize illustrated minor cards, the Marseille tarot, which predates Arthur Edward Waite's system, is designed quite simply and minimally, allowing cartomancers to utilize their understanding of suit-number combinations and their intuition when performing readings. In addition, we have in the Marseille tarot the addition of the knight to the sequence of court cards and the addition of the twenty-two cards known as the trump sequence, each depicting an earthly power, a spiritual truth, or a principle by which we may flourish or fail in our various endeavors. We shall explore the trumps, also called the "major arcana," more thoroughly in a devoted chapter since this progression of powers is complex and is worth examining on its own.

Whether working with playing cards or the tarot of Marseille, each number in a suit's sequence represents a convergence of forces. The number of the card represents one thing, and the suit itself represents another; together, they form an alignment of associations that renders a fuller picture. We will explore these convergences in more detail shortly, but for the sake of example, the four represents a stabilization of forces, while the heart (blood) represents love. Brought together in the four of hearts (or four of cups in Marseille), these might represent feelings of home, family, and being safe and grounded. Positioned negatively, this card might also represent feelings of boredom or entrapment in a stale relationship. Reading suit-number convergences is a bit like alchemy, but over time, interpreting these connections will become second-nature to the practiced witch.

While the number cards convey situations, the face cards convey personalities associated with motivations, goals, and desires. Each member of a royal family is driven by a particular pursuit, and this want, in conjunction with their suit, defines their character. This method differs substantially from other cartomantic approaches that would identify kings as men and queens as women, and this is for good reason. Because each face card is a personality, it would be incredibly limiting to identify those qualities as only belonging to one gender. Moreover, the querent (the one for whom the reading is being conducted) may express multiple qualities within them, and this is how the face cards can be read most effectively: as aspects or personalities that make up part of the querent's whole character rather than literal persons in a querent's life (though, conversely, they may also signify just that, depending on position and the reader's intuition).

The jokers belong in a class of their own outside of the cartomantic system. While most decks of playing cards today come with two jokers, this is only a fairly recent addition, historically speaking, so historic reproduction decks modeled after cards published before the 1900s will most likely not include this card. If the reader chooses to use jokers, they are not altogether dissimilar to The Fool of the tarot's major arcana, though with the additional connotations of a wild and unpredictable force, one best met with humor and a sense of adventure. The character depicted on many joker cards is derived by the carnival tradition of the King of Fools, and reaching even further back in time, to the Saturnalian reversal of caste roles and power structures. The joker can pose serious challenges, but he is, at heart, a trickster, and as such, can be seen as a devilish fingerprint left upon the playing card deck, Old Scratch's cameo appearance within his own picture book.

Red and Black Cards

The playing card deck is typically two-colored, and all cards in the deck can be divided between red and black. Though the illustrations in the Marseille tarot are more nuanced, we can still read similarities between rods and swords (clubs and spades), which are weaponry, and cups and coins (hearts and diamonds), which are meant to be consumed. It is in this divergence that we see echoes of old witch-lore and folkloric paganisms of the past, specifically to do with the mythic theme that has been called the "Oak King and Holly King" trope. We will return to a more in-depth analysis of this symbolism in a later portion of this book, but for now, let us explore how these two colors influence readings.

It is often the case that cartomantic systems reduce cards to "good" or "bad," but the problem with this reduction is two-fold: on the one hand, we risk projecting self-fulfilling prophecies of doom or boon upon the querent. On the other hand, we miss out on recognizing challenges appearing in card patterns as invitations for growth and change.

Red and black cards, rather, are best read as a spectrum balance of restoration and challenge. An abundance of red cards, which have to do with relationships and assets, can indicate a period of retreat and introspection in order to restore inner power and well-being. A wealth of black cards, which typically represent power dynamics and difficult trials, can indicate a phase of outward reaching, of meeting challenges head-on, and of being willing to change direction in order to respond to outside forces. As we will see, many red cards can still indicate pain and suffering, and many black cards can indicate joy and fulfillment. Rather than viewing cards as "bad" or "good," we can instead view each as complete and complex in and of itself. Even so, a predominance of color can and should help set the tone of the reading as one in which the querent should be reaching outward or inward.

The Four Suits

With the exception of jokers, the deck is divided into four suits: hearts or cups (identified in our rhyme as blood), spades or swords (knives), diamonds or coins (stones), and clubs or rods (crooks). Each of these represents an aspect of the querent's life.

Hearts speak to relationships, friendships, family, love, and our connections to others. These relationships can be fraught or harmonious, depending on the iteration of the number signs. An overwhelming presence of hearts in a reading signifies that relationships are at the heart of the matter at hand.

Spades are the most difficult suit. They represent challenges, trials, troubles, and conflict. Conversely, since it is only by suffering the new and unknown that we are able to grow, they represent evolution and learning. If many spades are on the table in a reading, the querent may be facing a particularly rough patch. This is best met with an openness to change and willingness to learn.

Diamonds are assets, but this can be a tricky suit. We typically think of assets as monetary or physical in nature, but this is often not the case. Our assets are the treasures we've acquired, both literal and figurative. For many of us, our intellect, skills, and learning can be our assets. For particularly manipulative, scheming persons, people can even be considered assets. What the querent considers their "treasures" may be open to interpretation. If the reading is overrun with diamonds, this is a time to think carefully about the resources at one's disposal and to use them wisely, whatever they may be.

Clubs speak to power and influence and those endeavors associated with these parts of life. Most people encounter power dynamics most frequently in a work environment through interactions with supervisors and subordinates, but power dynamics can also be encountered in legal matters, social situations, and creative projects. Whereas the hearts concern how people feel, clubs concern how people are put to work, how their effort is driven. A mass of clubs in a reading might signify ambitions at work.

Numerical Influences

The bulk of the deck is made up of

numbered cards. These iterations of one through ten speak to various circumstances in life that may express themselves through each of the suits. The skilled reader will be keen to observe that these powers may express themselves in a multitude of ways; rather than trying to memorize concrete circumstances like divorce or illness in association with a particular card, it is wise to consider the *transforming current* that underlies such an event and how that numeric force may express itself in each of the suits in various ways.

The aces most frequently represent beginnings or invitations. Depending on the position of this card in the spread, the querent may be invited to embrace a new chapter in life. The ace of diamonds, for instance, could represent a new financial opportunity or an opportunity to begin acquiring a new "asset" of some kind, which can often refer to a skill. In a negative or "releasing" position, this card may indicate the need to let go of a fledgling idea that just isn't going to come to fruition. Many aces indicate a wealth of new opportunities, but also a lack of grounding and connection to what came before. The querent may benefit from connecting new efforts to old ones so as not to throw the baby out with the bath-water.

The twos speak to pairings and partnerships. Most often, this involves two people, but it may also describe a querent experiencing ambivalence between two perspectives within themselves. For example, the two of hearts most frequently describes a relationship that is kind and loving (though not always). The two of spades might indicate a partnership or collaborative effort fraught with adversity and pain. A great many twos in a spread might signal the feeling of being stretched between many people demanding attention.

Three points form a triangle, the first stable shape that is also upward-reaching. Threes usually indicate a period of learning and exploration of some kind. Something is coming into its own and taking root, and the nature of that something will tell us if this is a favorable or unfavorable card. The three of clubs, for instance, may reveal a querent with social or occupational status on the rise. Depending on the position, it may also represent an opportunity for growth. A plethora of threes may tell us the querent is growing in many directions at once and might benefit from prioritizing efforts. In general, this is a favorable card and is sometimes referred to as the first of the "three harmonies," which also include the six and the nine.

The four, like a square made up of four points and four lines connecting them, represents stability. This can be positive if it represents something in which we desire stability, but it can also represent a state of stasis or stagnation. The four of diamonds can indicate financial stability, which is almost always a good thing; the four of spades represents a problem that simply won't go away, and this is rarely desirable. Challenges are necessary to feel alive, and the presence of too many fours can indicate a querent who feels "stuck."

The five topples the structure of the four. It is the first mobile shape: the pentagon. In the four, we have perfect symmetry; the five ruins this by throwing something unexpected into the mix. Fives communicate challenges and surprises, an element of chaos. The five of clubs might mean the destabilization of something at one's workplace or profession that requires a new approach. The five of hearts can indicate a potentially troublesome change in a relationship. Although the five is one of two discord cards (the other discord being the seven), the five is the lesser of the two and usually represents a challenge that can be overcome. These are often moments of learning and growth disguised as unpleasant circumstances. The five is best met with courage and flexibility, a willingness to try something new.

In the six, we return to the symmetry of the four, but now, we have sufficient points to form a cube, a shape that is three-dimensional, stable, and full of harmony. Something is not only growing, but ready to be harvested. It has finally taken form. This is often related to an effort sown in the querent's past. For example, the six of diamonds may signal that a past debt of some kind is about to be repaid or an investment of time and effort returned. A great deal of sixes in a spread may be a strong suggestion that the querent seize opportunities now before they rot on the vine. The harvest cannot wait. This is the second of the three cards referred to as "the three harmonies," and it is usually a good sign.

The seven brings us to the more sinister of the cards known as the "two discords." Although the five represented a challenging surprise, the seven's offering is poisonous and wicked. Here lies cruelty, malice, and selfish impulse at the expense of others. This is not an opportunity, but a trap. If the numerical force of the six formed a harmonious cube, this is a box with something dreadful tucked inside. Faced with an overwhelming number of sevens, the querent may feel anxious, but rest assured that the wickedness of the seven can almost always be weathered or overcome. If many sevens are here, now is a time to be on the lookout for malice and to treat others with an extra measure of kindness, just in case the wickedness of this card is unintentionally our own.

Eights are like wheels. They bring movement, change, and journeys. The force of the eight in the suit of hearts can be exhilarating with its suggestion of new infatuations and sexual exploits; the eight of diamonds less so, especially for a querent already nervous about finances. If too many of these unruly eights turn up in a spread, the querent might be encouraged to slow down and consider carefully before acting.

At last, we come to the nine. Here we encounter the final iteration of the "three harmonies." In the six, we were able to reap previously sown efforts; in the nine, we have a bounty greater than we could have hoped for. This is the sudden windfall, the unforeseen romance, the remission of disease. It's always more than we feel we deserve, and this is the strange challenge of the nine: feeling worthy. It's harder than it sounds. Can the querent release enough defensiveness, doubt, and insecurity to accept the gift of the nine? For many people, especially those who have experienced trauma, joy and success can be terrifying things. If we're too rigid and callous, lady luck may simply move on to the next lucky person. So much for our happy ending.

The ten is a fascinating card because it represents both the culmination of a suit and an ending, much akin to a kind of graduation. Something has been completed, and though it will always be a part of us, we must turn our attention towards something new to avoid becoming ghosts of our past. It can also represent finally arriving at a goal or at the pinnacle of some peak we once set out to climb. Too many tens in a spread can indicate grief for something that is now finished. Trying to hold on to it will only result in pain and entrapment.

The Royal Families

As previously noted, each of the face cards in the playing card deck represents a personality that is often an aspect of the querent. Depending on position, the querent may be counseled to embrace or release a particular power within themselves.

Jacks or knaves, conveyed as pages in Marseille, represent learning and seeking. The jack is on a journey to become something and is willing to embrace vulnerability and fallibility in order to learn. The jack is imperfect, but accepts that as part of growth. He is also the most joyful and enraptured of the face cards because he sees the force of his particular suit with fresh and unjaded eyes.

Queens represent wisdom, craft, and cunning. Although the king imagines himself to be the most mighty, it is the queen who pulls the strings behind the scenes. She can see what lies ahead and is perceptive of others' emotions and intentions. She relies on her experience and shrewd sensibilities to make wise choices. This wisdom may express itself as ice-cold manipulation in the spades suit or as insightful empathy in the hearts suit. Because she is more inclined to thinking and talking, the queen can sometimes lack motivation and effort.

Kings value force and might. They have the largest egos and are prone to trampling on toes, but they are also the card most inclined to action and results. The king can make things happen, though his ham-fisted tactics may not accomplish his goals in the most careful way. The King of Hearts wants to be loved and acts from this need, but without the wisdom of the queen, the results are less than pleasant.

Because part of our goal is to identify a system integrating cartomantic methods using playing cards and Marseille tarot, we must here address one of the two chief differences between the two: the appearance of the knight. We can easily identify the knave or jack of the playing card deck with the page in the tarot deck since they serve a similar role in the court and even appear similar in their illustrated forms. The knight, however, is distinct in the tarot court system, comprising a more active principle than the queen and king, who do not engage in battle directly, and a loftier position than the page or knave. In feudalist systems, knights would be portioned some share of wealth and land, and so their military role would have granted them a somewhat elevated position.

As the single court card most associated with military engagement and violence, the knight can, like the king, represent power, but in a different light. While the king seeks power in order to rule over a kingdom (the desire for power), following the vision of what he imagines to be the most beneficial creed of the land (regardless of the fact that it may not actually benefit anyone since the king is ultimately ego-driven), the knight seeks power purely for power's sake. We can view him as a more violent and volatile expression of the reach for power, seeking to assume a higher position and status, but not necessarily considering the long-term ramifications of his actions in terms of actual leadership. At the same time, however, he is less desirous of owning and manipulating others, so we cannot simply describe him as a "worse" version of the king. Perhaps most simply, he is the aggressive and self-empowered impulse to action, regardless of the consequences.

A Card-by-Card Analysis

It is in the intersection of suit and numerical influences that we find the keys to interpreting individual cards, and though the meaning of an individual card hinges strongly on its position and proximity to other cards within a spread, each can also be said to contain its own world, its own unique flavor that may express itself in various ways within a particular reading. Following the guidelines in "The Devil's Picture-Book," our mnemonic poem from the beginning of this text, we can discern the properties at work at the intersection of sign and suit for each. Let us explore the cards individually, then, bearing in mind that spread, position, and the intuition of a particular reader will also color the effects of any card—like light pouring through a stained-glass window.

Ace of Hearts (Ace of Cups in Marseille)
Ace to start the journey...
Blood to cherish loved ones...

We begin our journey through the suit of relationships and emotional ties with a complex card. Aces tend to indicate the new and unexpected, an initiation of sorts, and at the beginning of any journey, we must ask two questions. First, what is the goal? In the suit of blood, we begin an adventure in order to seek fulfillment in connection with others. This can certainly represent a new romantic interest and the desire to satisfy new love's urges, but don't be fooled; this card can also suggest something as simple as a new friendship or a new beginning in any kind of existing relationship between people. In the presence of many spades or clubs, this card may even indicate a new relationship fraught with toxicity or odd power dynamics. Read in an advisory capacity, this card tells us to be willing to begin a relationship (or renew an existing one) with a clean slate, free of any grievances or regrets from the past.

Two of Hearts (Two of Cups in Marseille)
Two to make a pair...
Blood to cherish loved ones...

The focus of the two in all its iterations is

on the "back-and-forth" of conversations, negotiations, and relationships of all kinds. In hearts, the suit of blood, this principle is expressed in the form of relationships with a strong bond. In previous ages, this might indicate marriage or the bond between two married people, but we better understand now that powerful relationships can exist in many different forms outside of marriage. The two of hearts might even represent a deep friendship or strong familial bond. Note that the relationship indicated by this card is not always a healthy or functional one. The prerequisite suggested by this card is merely that it is rooted in a strong bond, and as anyone who has been in a harmful relationship can tell you, love is not always enough. In its ideal state, though, this card can indicate a mutual devotion that lasts and provides fulfillment. As a card of action, this card suggests that we renew our commitment to someone we care for and pay careful attention to the balance of what is given and what is taken between two loving parties.

Three of Hearts (Three of Cups in Marseille)

Three, a sapling growing...
Blood to cherish loved ones...

We are well on our way now through the suit of emotions and ties. In the first of the three harmonies (the other two being sixes and nines), we find the principle of increase bringing about an energetic peak in the energy of the suit of blood. This "increase" can express itself in a number of ways: an intense infatuation to someone, an exciting new sexual relationship, a vivifying experience that renews one's vigor and lust for life and love, a sudden boom in popularity, or even the tingle of anticipation for a party or other social event. The three of hearts captures all of these and more because its central energy concerns the thrill and electricity of social interaction in its many facets. Later in the suit, this energy will be grounded and fulfilled in more stable forms, but for now, it is volatile, but generally benign, suggestive of good-natured adventures and escapades. Read in its advisory aspect, this card asks that we allow ourselves to experience the thrill of new growth alongside others, to experience relationships with the vigor and intensity that we typically feel in our youth.

Four of Hearts (Four of Cups in Marseille)

Four, a stable chair...
Blood to cherish loved ones...

    The grounding and stabilizing influence of the four is expressed uniquely in the suit of hearts, which is, by its very nature, more fluid and enigmatic than the other suits due to its emotional subject. Bringing stability to the slippery, complex world of relationships and feelings can take us in two directions. On the one hand, it may bring a welcome sense of security, as in a relationship full of trust and reliability. This condition of stability can allow love to grow and flourish since it need no longer worry about being abandoned or betrayed. On the other hand, taking a relationship for granted can lead to stagnation, boredom, and feeling trapped. If the four is a chair, then that chair must be more than a place to sit. Let us consider it an antique chair carved of some rare wood, ornate in detail, its seat and back upholstered and embroidered. It allows us to rest securely and to feel supported, but it must also be beautiful and worthy of polishing, cleaning, and upkeep. The four of hearts asks all of this of us: to feel and enjoy the secure embrace that grounds us, but to repay that security with appreciation and devotion in kind.

Five of Hearts (Five of Cups in Marseille)
Five to throw the carriage...
Blood to cherish loved ones...

In the suit of blood, the first of the two discords brings forth what we might call a lesser evil than that represented by the seven. Unlike its sister, the five is not malevolent, only careless and capricious. Its function is to disrupt the stability of the four, to complicate what was once orderly and balanced with an element of surprise that may end up playing out for good or for ill, depending on how we approach it. This could express itself as a new, unpredictable party in a group of friends, a period of separation between lovers, a secret revealed between people who once trusted one another, or an argument that accidentally goes just a hair too far with harsh words. These are events that challenge relationships, but can, if approached with care, grow the bond even stronger, as metal is tempered with heat. Alternatively, if the love and care are insufficient, the five can reveal that insufficiency for all to see by putting us to the test, laying bare those incongruities so that we may make a new choice for the betterment of ourselves and for others. Consider, then, that the five is a crucible from which nothing can emerge unchanged, but that the change in question will always bring us closer to the truest form, to the bare naked truth that lies underneath, which may result in some temporary pain, but is usually for the better as long as we can perceive what is happening and act with wisdom. This is a time for honesty and the stating of our needs and desires with others, which may result in one or more parties walking away, at least for a time. But if there is love at the root of the bond, it is also a time for kindness and renewal.

Six of Hearts (Six of Cups in Marseille)
Six to gather grain...
Blood to cherish loved ones...

Now do we arrive at the second of the three harmonies, this one indicating a time to gather the fruit that began to grow in the sign of the three. It has now reached its maturity and is ready to give back twice the energy it borrowed on its adventures. In hearts, the suit of blood, this often takes the form of loved ones rallying to support us in our time of need, relatives repaying kindnesses with kindness, lovers celebrating years of faithful togetherness, and all of the treasures that come of investing our time and energy in the people we love by showing them what they mean to us. If the five has tested those bonds, then the six reveals us to truly reap what we sow in matters of the heart. In a darker aspect, this can mean grievances returned upon us, but even in this, there is a lesson, for it wipes the board clean and allows us to build something new, those debts now repaid. Most often, the six of hearts gives us permission to call on our loved ones, to rely on others, and to permit them to cherish us as we have cherished them.

Seven of Hearts (Seven of Cups in Marseille)
Seven spelling wickedness...
Blood to cherish loved ones...

Sevens are complex in that their wickedness stems from self-service, and in the suit of feelings and bonds, this complexity is exacerbated. This card can signify an emotionally disturbed person who seeks to cause pain for the pleasure it causes them. There are no winners in this game of blood, for all parties will be cut by the seven's razor-sharp sword. But while there can be no victory, there can usually be some form of escape; as with most contagious toxicities, the seven's energy here will simply turn inward, falling back on the wicked party if they can find no victim, for the difficult truth here is that this figure is merely the carrier of this contagion and rarely has a sense of control over it. On the other hand, this card can represent the need for self-care and a focus on the self. If the seven's toxicity is rooted in the vacuum formed by the wounded self, then the answer lies in attention paid inward rather than outward. What may present as negative feelings aimed at an outside party are truly rooted within ourselves, and we must release the curse there, within the walls of our own heart, and heal ourselves before we can engage meaningfully with others.

Eight of Hearts (Eight of Cups in Marseille)
Eight to take the reins...
Blood to cherish loved ones...

We have survived the storm of the seven of hearts, and now we come to a new leg of the journey, like travelers fleeing dire straits. The wagon on which we ride is perhaps rickety, and the strange horse may be taking us any number of places, but the eight grants us a sense of self-sufficiency, and so we welcome our refreshing view of the countryside. All things change with time, and in the suit of blood, changes in relationships can be many things. In long-lasting relationships, we become many different people over the years as we continue to evolve, and we must accept that we are, in a sense, "along for the ride" with our loved ones as they grow and change alongside us. Before us lies some sort of adventure, less dangerous than we see in the five, though not without risk. The traveler across the seas can easily fall prey to culture shock and become homesick, longing for some version of the past preserved in memory. The suit of blood is sentimental, and so we must try to remember that change is natural. We must welcome it even as it pains us, and we must find some way of admiring it, of appreciating some beauty in our view from our little wagon on the dusty road. After all, if we allow our loved ones to change, then so, too, are we allowed the same privilege, permitted to become a new person any day of our lives, to reinvent ourselves and our relationships as need be, regardless of how old we are or what pains we have endured. We are always free, and so we must allow others their freedoms in kind.

Nine of Hearts (Nine of Cups in Marseille)
Nine, a cornucopia...
Blood to cherish loved ones...

As the last and ultimate of the three harmonies, the cornucopia of the nine finds itself at its most vivacious and celebrated in the suit of blood. Here is the feast of the heart, the fulfillment of emotional and sensual needs, and in fact, a sense of loving and belonging and satisfaction beyond what we even imagine possible for ourselves. This is love overflowing, relationships prospering, being seen and celebrated for exactly who we are. This is being loved deeply, down to the dark corners of ourselves we perhaps imagined unlovable. There can be some degree of pain in this, for in order to accept the nine's cornucopia, we must admit to loving ourselves insufficiently, to growing used to insufficiency and perhaps even "settling" for less love than we deserved. These admissions hurt because what we once considered merely our fair circumstances are now revealed as hardships, and we are forced to face those wounds as if they are fresh. If we can rise to this occasion, those pains can now be truly healed; not forgotten, but no longer held, much like an old photograph that may now be set in its album and placed on a shelf. We know now, that we are utterly loved and that we are worthy of that love. This card does come, as most do, with its own word of caution, for the feast of the heart is meant to be shared. Hoarding this newfound attention and appreciation all to ourselves can result in narcissism and egomania, and so all of this love pouring upon us must also pour through us in order to nourish others.

Ten of Hearts (Ten of Cups in Marseille)
Ten, completion's crown...
Blood to cherish loved ones...

If the ten is a crown, then in the suit of emotions and ties, it is an illustrious one indeed, granting us hard-won emotional wisdom and the perspective to understand and endure the challenges and temptations of this suit. On a literal level, this card can represent the ending of a relationship or its "graduation" to a new and more beneficial form. If we read deeper, however, we see that this card can also indicate the heart tempered by experience. We are no longer the naïve lover, the new kid in town, the self-doubting child, or the presumptuous suitor. We have seen some or many of these iterations in our journey through love's many roads, and though we have been weathered by some of them, we have also been inspired and fulfilled by others. We can see quickly through the lies and manipulations of those who would use us, and we can recognize a true and kind heart when we see it, even if it is dressed in rags and speaks harshly. We understand the emotional needs of those around us and how to nourish those bonds. But tens always imagine themselves complete, and this sense of finality in the suit of the heart risks ennui. Experience is always the best teacher, but if we truly believe that we have "seen it all" when it comes to love, we risk becoming jaded, like an old blues singer crooning about love won and lost. The solution to the ten's nihilism is, of course, to begin again at one. We must take this wisdom and apply it, beginning a new journey, renewing ourselves, and using that hard-won knowledge to make better choices this time around.

Jack of Hearts (Page of Cups in Marseille)

Jacks are ever-learning...
Blood to cherish loved ones...

This person, or more often, aspect of the querent, is what we might call the "student of love." Naïve and child-like, the knave can be foolish and can make mistakes with ease, but if these are made in the name of learning, then none can be considered a complete tragedy. Here we find the lover who clings too tightly out of fear of abandonment, the partner who cheats instead of speaking openly about their needs, but more often, we find the dewy-eyed romantic who is simply "in love with love." Often, this figure speaks to a sense of joy and child-like wonder, which is why, despite his inexperience, he is more likely to land on his feet than the knaves of other suits. His innocence endears him to others and often protects him from the consequences of his choices. The Jack has much to learn, but if he knows this and accepts it, then the road before him is full of adventure instead of merely danger. It takes time and experience to know what makes us emotionally happy and fulfilled, and this character epitomizes that learning experience, which is best embraced with humility, humor, and an open heart.

Simplified cartomantic systems interpret the Jack of Hearts as Cancer, the cardinal sign of water, and as an aspect of the querent's personality.

Queen of Hearts (Queen of Cups in Marseille)
Queens are ever-wise...
Blood to cherish loved ones...

The Queen of Hearts, being wise in matters of the heart, is the ultimate master of this suit. Though we might imagine the wisdom of love as a character of unending gentleness and compassion, it may surprise us to find that she is equally stern and discerning. To be emotionally wise certainly encompasses kindness, but it also encompasses setting healthy boundaries, intuiting the manipulative attempts of others, and practicing self-love as a true discipline. In truth, her gift is that of a seer. The queen's charge is not to surrender to the emotional demands of everyone who crosses her path, but to protect her heart and those hearts she cherishes while being reasonably open to change and the shifting of feelings over time. Given a difficult situation between people, she will always try to discern the path that causes the least amount of suffering while allowing the most room for fulfillment of all parties involved, and because she can see inside the hearts of others without trying, this is easy work. While the king seeks to control love and use it to elevate his own stature, it is the queen who truly rules her kingdom, for she can predict the machinations of the king at every turn and either avoid or redirect his efforts as she chooses. She perhaps views him as an amusing, if pitiful companion who wastes too much time trying to control the hearts of others instead of tending to his own. Simplified cartomantic systems interpret the Queen of Hearts as Pisces, the mutable sign of water, and as an aspect of the querent's personality.

King of Hearts (King of Cups in Marseille)
Kings seek to gain power...
Blood to cherish loved ones...

Pity the King of Hearts. What he desires most is to be adored, admired, and enshrined in the hearts of his people, but because he is driven by power rather than wisdom, he mistakes transactional exchanges of social currency for real love. The kingdom he manifests is one of carefully pontificated social moves and actions, and he philosophizes and debates every party invitation, every choice of furniture in his halls, every discussion with other leaders in excruciating detail. On the surface, his kingdom is full of care and social niceties, but we must look closer. In treating other people as his emotional battery propelling his narcissism, he is locked in a pattern of taking from others endlessly without giving back, and in doing so, he forever misses the lesson: that in matters of the heart, we are only ever fulfilled when giving and taking are brought into balance, when we allow ourselves to be as vulnerable as we ask others to be. The king believes that what he needs to be fulfilled is the devotion and admiration of others, to be the apple of every eye, to paint his imagined enemies as monsters to be feared and himself as a hero to be worshipped, but this is a cage he builds for himself, for he has mistaken flattery and the winning of popularity contests with real love, and so his thirst can never be truly sated, no matter how many hearts he collects for his court. Simplified cartomantic systems interpret the King of Hearts as Scorpio, the fixed sign of water, and as an aspect of the querent's self.

Knight of Cups (Marseille)

As a more volatile expression of power within the suit of emotions and ties, the knight of cups is both a romantic and what we might call a player. He knows his power to bend the emotions of others, and he chases the thrill of sexual and romantic escapades blindly, running from one target to the next. What he seeks most of all is to test the limits of his powers, to see how many hearts he can win over, but unlike the king, he is not building a kingdom, so there is no need for care and deliberation in his wild pursuits. This knight is not necessarily malevolent, though; he simply has yet to understand the reality of the pain he causes in his actions as he is too absorbed in the electrifying thrill of the chase.

Ace of Spades (Ace of Swords in Marseille)
Ace to start the journey...
A knife to joys divide...

In this journey's beginning, there is already woe early in the path. This suit's influence on the ace darkens its initiating energy, resulting in a threshold crossed through with dread, perhaps upon a road we imagine can lead only to suffering.

But the only suffering here is that which we have brought with us, and the curse is of course of our own design. The ace is meant to be whole and unified, a newborn simple and pure before the vast complexity of the world, unhindered by expectations or presumptions, but the suit of knives divides us against ourselves, filling us with inner conflict. We do not trust our own feet that carry us on these first steps, and so, like a self-fulfilling prophecy, we will arrive where we imagine. In its advisory capacity, this card asks us to begin the true journey, the deep journey, the one in which we gaze courageously at the conflicts and darkness within ourselves in order to make room for true resolution.

Two of Spades (Two of Swords in Marseille)
Two to make a pair...
A knife to joys divide...

What can be done to help this conflicted pair of progress along the path? Spades bring us trials and tribulations, often in the world of labor and work, and so this card can signify a difficult working relationship. While the two of hearts presents us with an effort at balance, a give and take in measure, the two of spades is a stalemate. No deal will be reached. No trade will be made. No peace will last. But perhaps, if we look closely, we can see that there are no villains here at all, that both sides feel strongly because both are right in their stance. Each of these powerful perspectives deserves its own movement and action, but they must each find another to engage with in order to experience progress towards their goals. Perhaps when they accomplish this, they will realize that they were never true enemies at all.

Three of Spades (Three of Swords in Marseille)
Three, a sapling growing...
A knife to joys divide...

The first of the three harmonies brings a moment of relief to this suit, for while there is challenge, it becomes clear now that the conflicts we bravely face will have an end, that we are making some incremental progress towards a resolution. Perhaps a meeting has finally been scheduled to resolve a conflict at work, or perhaps a missing piece of a vexing problem has finally come to light. There is still much work to be done to resolve the source of the problem, for certain, but what can be said now is that there is a visible light at the end of the tunnel. Our efforts are not, as we perhaps once imagined, wasted, and we are not as trapped as we once imagined ourselves to be. What we must decide now is if the increased effort and toil here are worth the reward that will come, for the suit of knives is still a difficult journey, and we must be sure that the price we pay will be worth the suffering in the end. If we decide to move forward, we can be sure that success is possible if we stay the path and endure the trials that come.

Four of Spades (Four of Swords in Marseille)
Four, a stable chair...
A knife to joys divide...

At the convergence of the four's stasis and the knife suit's churning conflict, we can read two possible scenarios. This card can sometimes indicate a respite in a period of conflict, a moment of resting in the eye of the storm. This is, unfortunately, a temporary state, and the time of rest must be used to regain strength for the continuation of conflict ahead, or perhaps to plan one's next move in order to reach a swifter resolution to the vexing problems at hand.

Conversely, we can read the four of spades as a problem that simply will not budge, a woe that has the lasting, stable power of the four, bearing its weight upon us like a great block of stone. In this case, it is best to walk away rather than waste the effort trying to change the unchangeable. Whether we read this as a period of rest or an immovable problem will depend on the reader's first instinct and the relationship between this card and others in the spread.

Five of Spades (Five of Swords in Marseille)
Five to throw the carriage...
A knife to joys divide...

If the five, as our first discord, represents a toppling chaotic energy, then it is usually a very unwelcome card in the suit of conflicts, toil, and division. Powers that were once matched in stalemate are now unleashed in full force, and previous agreements are now thrown aside in the name of "might is right." There is an opportunity here, however, to avoid and redirect this fitful current of change, for the energy of the five is wild and short-sighted, and these problems may end up counteracting each other, enabling us to slip away unnoticed (for a time). Whether this expresses itself as interdepartmental conflicts at work or spats between relatives, this is a time to avoid getting involved. When the dust has settled, we will most likely find that something useful for resolution has been brought to light, but for now, we must stand back and let the storm rage on.

Six of Spades (Six of Swords in Marseille)
Six to gather grain...
A knife to joys divide...

We finally arrive at the second of our three harmonies in this difficult suit, and just as we foresaw in the three, there is now a clear road to resolution. Some old debt is now repaid, and the path to peace and serenity becomes much more clear. Our efforts at achieving a solution to a long-standing problem have proved fruitful, though we may have paid a dear price for it. Can we accept the terms of this compromise? Is it fair? Will this resolution give us the things we need to feel fulfilled and put this conflict (either inner or outer) to rest? If the answer is yes, then we can finally breathe deeply and begin to imagine a better future for ourselves. If the answer is no, then we must be willing to return to the wild torrents we survived in the five of spades and allow the storm to rage on until the true source of the problem reveals itself.

Seven of Spades (Seven of Swords in Marseille)
Seven spelling wickedness...
A knife to joys divide...

Thank goodness there are few cards as menacing as the seven of spades. The currents of the seven and the spade are both cruel, and in their culmination, we see a uniquely dark card that rarely indicates anything good. Here we find cruelty, suffering, and tragedy: the boss who delights in tormenting his staff, the sudden illness that throws our health and our lives into chaos, the storm that causes devastating damage to our home. There is no reasoning with the seven of spades, but if hope exists, it is in the fact that this card represents a "rock bottom" situation in which things simply cannot get worse than they already are. Now that we have seen the root of this hardship, we can face it head-on and make new choices. Often, there is a boldness that comes with facing the seven of spades. When we are pushed against a wall with nothing left to lose, we find what we are made of and often surprise ourselves with our own ferocity in the face of this monster. Although things may be dire and bleak, there is some cold comfort in the fact that there is nothing left to fear, no more enemies to be revealed. Here is the true form of the conflict we face, leaving nothing left for us to dread or worry over. Now is the time to protect what is ours, to stand up for ourselves, to defend what we hold dear. The seven's inward focus can strengthen us, if we let it. Let us muster all of our might and face it with courage.

Eight of Spades (Eight of Swords in Marseille)
Eight to take the reins...
A knife to joys divide...

The change initiated by the eight relieves the pressure we experienced in the seven of spades, allowing us to reimagine ourselves and our circumstances. What might life look like without this long-standing curse that has plagued our thoughts all this time? We can now imagine ourselves without it since we have faced its darkness head-on, but trauma is tricky, and the actual process of releasing this pain we have kept is an incremental experience. As we begin new journeys and change directions in our lives, we often find ourselves haunted by old pain, and the challenge we face is to make new decisions uninfluenced by the pain we have endured. If we simply avoid the road that previously caused us woe, then the journey is merely a form of escape, a constant running that will ultimately lead us back to our pain. Instead, we must choose from joy, imagining a more fulfilled version of ourselves and acting to achieve that goal.

Nine of Spades (Nine of Swords in Marseille)
Nine, a cornucopia...
A knife to joys divide...

This last harmony in the suit of spades is suggestive of a rallying of forces on our behalf. Along our journey of woes and toil, we have been forced to engage new parts of ourselves, to build new muscles and call upon new allies. Now, those resources outmatch the darkness we once faced. This is usually an unexpected turn of events, since we entered this difficult journey reluctantly and full of dread, but now we see that there were always powers on our side of the fight, and that the figurative monster we battled never stood a chance. The seeds of resolution we sowed in the three and harvested in the nine are now a feast before us: a triumph sure and certain over what seemed an insurmountable foe. May we never forget the lesson here; it is never too late to make the effort, for the journey is long, and the seeds we plant will eventually bring forth the bounty.

Ten of Spades (Ten of Swords in Marseille)
Ten, completion's crown...
A knife to joys divide...

At last, the ten of spades: proof of our old curses being dispelled, our monsters vanquished, our wounds healed. Here lie the remains of what once plagued us, and this card is its funeral. Not only have we conquered the suit of trials and tribulations, but we have emerged better somehow, for the friends we called upon for aid and the lessons we gained in battling this darkness have actually made us more prepared, more ready for future challenges. We are stronger than we imagined ourselves able to be, steadier, grittier. We know now that we can weather seemingly impossible circumstances. Now begins the difficult work of releasing the ghost of the curse, of allowing it to be finally put to rest for good. This goodbye can be painful because we have been forced to invent combative and survivalist parts of ourselves in order to endure our trials, and we have grown accustomed to our callouses and our weaponry. The time for them, though, has passed, and if we want to life a fulfilling life, we must be willing to release them. If not, we risk becoming merely the shell of our previous pain, a museum erected to the memory of the worst moments of our lives. Can we let it go now? Can we make room for what is new?

Jack of Spades (Page of Swords in Marseille)
Jacks are ever-learning...
A knife to joys divide...

Our poor knave's journey is always one of learning, but in this suit, what he must learn is the darkness of the world: its cruelty, its malice, its hardships, its endless toil. Parents seek to protect their children from being exposed to the realities of death, violence, and hardship too early in life, but the Jack of Spades' lesson is precisely this: to come to accept that all things must suffer, labor, and eventually die, that hardship is not a momentary discomfort experienced by him alone, but a ubiquitous condition of existence, as regular as the seasons. In learning this lesson, this young idealist will learn compassion for others as well as appreciation for the moments of beauty and joy that make up the other seasons of a life. In practical terms, this can represent a person coming to grips with tragedy or loss or a person trying to understand a challenge placed before them. Our knave needs comfort, for certain, but more importantly, he needs the truth, for this is the only thing that can allow him to move beyond his bewilderment. Simplified cartomantic systems interpret this card as Gemini, the cardinal sign of air, and as an aspect of the querent's own personality.

Queen of Spades (Queen of Swords in Marseille)
Queens are ever wise...
A knife to joys divide...

Our dark queen has both studied at and graduated from the school of trials and tribulations. She understands the darkness inherent in the world and how to face it with courage. From her deep understanding comes her most poignant and unique quality among the court cards, for of all of the personalities before us, she is most without fear. Nothing will frighten her or cause her to waiver in pursuit of her goals. She does not entertain delusions and has little tolerance for liars, flatterers, and tall tales. Her mind is precise and calculating, and because she is always prepared for the worst possible outcome, she at all times says what she means and means exactly what she says. None should call the dark queen's bluff, for she does not lie. Surprisingly, though she does not advertise this as her strong suit, she has a skill for guiding others through difficult times in their lives, for while she is brutally honest, she does not allow us to paint the picture darker than it actually is, forcing us to take a fair assessment of our might and our resources in the face of adversity. Simplified cartomantic systems designate this card as Libra, the mutable sign of air, and an aspect of the querent's personality.

King of Spades (King of Swords in Marseille)
Kings seek to gain power...
A knife to joys divide...

There is no tip-toeing around the fact that the King of Spades is a tyrant. He uses intimidation and threats (be they overt or implied) in order to control every member of his kingdom. He is feared instead of being loved, obeyed instead of being adored. But beneath his actions lie motivations that are not altogether evil. What our dark king desires most is to protect his kingdom from the ruin and devastation that he imagines comes from stepping out of line and defying the status quo. Though his means are disturbing, his intentions are to protect and to provide security. He does not understand the lesson that the queen has already mastered: that we can never be completely certain of safety, security, and protection in this life, and so we must be honest with ourselves at all times and be willing to take actions when the need arises. In short, in an effort to save his kingdom from suffering and pain, our king ends up preventing anyone from truly living, and in the process, causes more woe than he means to circumvent. Simplified cartomantic systems equate this card with Aquarius, the fixed sign of air, and with an aspect of the querent's personality.

Knight of Swords (Marseille)

It isn't that our knight of swords enjoys attacking others constantly; it's simply that he isn't sure how to stop doing it. To him, the road to achievement lies in conquering others, and he sees this pattern in the world all around him. Anything and everything is a competition. In order to justify his aggression, he often adopts some disguise of righteousness, reframing his barbarism as a crusade against some imaginary evil or other, but in his heart, he simply enjoys the fight. This energy can be put to productive use if he can be guided to conquer his own inner beasts rather than the ones he perceives around him. This work, if he can be coaxed in such a direction, will transform his bloodthirst into strategy, his aggression into a love of tactics. He will never be a "big picture" sort of person, but he can learn to be very effective at setting up a series of tasks and executing them with finesse, and so he can become more tolerable with the right sort of coaching.

Ace of Diamonds (Ace of Coins in Marseille)
Ace to start the journey...
Stone to keep all treasures...

Some perceive the suit of diamonds as pertaining to more mundane matters than hearts or spades, but this isn't always true. While diamonds certainly concern financial matters a good deal of the time, the heart of this suit lies in our "treasures," whatever we may believe those to be. These things can be our homes, our gardens, our families, our skill sets, our academic pedigrees, our spiritual practices, etc. What unites and defines our various "treasures" is that we build and accrue them over time, that they are hard-won and valued by the querent. In our ace, we begin a journey to acquire some asset of some kind, which could indicate a new business, a new academic program, a job offer, a purchase, or some acquisition of some valued thing. This card bodes well for such affairs, so long as we are patient and willing to put wait for the things that matter to us. The suit of diamonds itself is suited to slow and steady growth, but is not often indicative of sudden and volatile wealth.

Two of Diamonds (Two of Coins in Marseille)
Two to make a pair...
Stone to keep all treasures...

As an iteration of the two, this card is

indicative of arrangements, agreements, and partnerships, but in its station within the suit of assets and accruals, it is revealed to pertain best to dealmaking. A pact made carefully should carry benefits for both parties and losses for both parties, otherwise, the balancing nature of the two is toppled, and this card loses its favorable connotations. Now is a time for considering carefully what will be offered and in exchange for what reward, to ensure that arrangements result in agreeable prosperity all around. Selling a home at a financial loss, for instance, is a difficult road to walk, but if the home in question requires maintenance and upkeep that we simply cannot manage, then we are gaining something from this deal that matters little to the other party, but perhaps a great deal to us: more time to spend on other matters. In terms of relationships, this may indicate a good time to reevaluate ground rules and expectations. At work, we may find ourselves positioned for partnerships that are profitable. All of this is contingent upon taking a careful inventory of what matters to us and forging agreements that are expressed clearly in advance.

Three of Diamonds (Three of Coins in Marseille)

Three, a sapling growing...
Stone to keep all treasures...

Harmonies express themselves beautifully in the suit of treasures, and as the first of these, the three indicates the early stages of a planned project that will take much time to come to fruition. Remember that diamonds are slow and not swift; the heaviness of stone takes time to move. Nonetheless, something we began in the one is now beginning to take form in the three, and the possibilities are enticing. Under the influence of the three of diamonds, we fall asleep fantasizing about the prospects of this project's culmination, visualizing all of the dreams that may be within reach if we can simply stay the course. The signs are clear that we are on the right track, but we cannot simply allow our efforts to go on autopilot. Forming clear deadlines and other kinds of long-term planning would be an excellent use of this card's energies, translating the excitement we feel into concrete steps to continue building on what we have begun.

Four of Diamonds (Four of Coins in Marseille)
Four, a stable chair...

Stone to keep all treasures...

The four of diamonds is a hefty card full of inertia, though that may take different forms depending on the reader's intuition and the card's placement within the spread. Met with the immovable nature of the four, the suit of assets can express contentedness and security, allowing us to relax our guard and enjoy the gains we have made, to pause for a moment in our studies or our work to simply bask in the feeling of having enough of whatever it is we set out to accrue. Think of the hard-working restauranteur who has worked for years to finally achieve a profit and is now able to enjoy a short vacation. Conversely, this card can sometimes signify greediness and the hoarding of resources that are meant to be shared with others, like the billionaire who has more money than he can ever spend but still insists on a sky-high salary for himself as his lowest paid workers struggle to afford the basic cost of living. If our wealth-hoarder were willing to spread this prosperity fairly, he would still have enough wealth, but he would also have the invaluable resources of his workers' admiration and loyalty. When we cling too greedily to one form of treasure, we sometimes neglect others, allowing them to slip through our fingers in our blindness.

Five of Diamonds (Five of Coins in Marseille)
Five to throw the carriage...
Stone to keep all treasures...

The five is a nasty number in this suit. Because diamonds are naturally inclined towards slow and careful growth, the chaotic energy of this number is felt more severely, like a spark allowed to land in a barn full of hay. Something has been allowed to go haywire, and the results are terribly disappointing: set-backs in academic progress, financial losses in a business, being passed over for a promotion, and all manner of projects gone awry. It's no one's fault, of course, since our first discord never means to cause anyone pain, but its impact is felt sharply nonetheless. What once felt like sure success is now called into question, challenged by unforeseen circumstances. As with all fives, though, this can be a lesson that results in greater growth since it reveals hidden instabilities. The house that we once thought sturdy is now discovered to have some foundation issues, and though we are disappointed, it is ultimately better that we know now and are able plan accordingly. Next time, we will adjust our assumptions, and we will be more prepared.

Six of Diamonds (Six of Coins in Marseille)
Six to gather grain...
Stone to keep all treasures...

Long ago (or at least what may feel like long ago), we began to lay the groundwork for a dream, and now, we can finally pluck the first fruits of its harvest. Perhaps we have finally finished a lengthy training program or written that novel. Something, somewhere, has come to fruition, and the time is right to reach for it. This card tells us "the time is now," and it often comes as a surprise in readings when it arrives. The progress of diamonds-related activities can feel so slow that we often forget the seeds we planted so long ago, having perhaps thought it too far-fetched that our goals would ever be achieved. This moment calls for looking back at efforts spent in the past and calling in those debts to be repaid, for now is the ideal moment to finally have the prize. On the other hand, sometimes we find that we have achieved what we set out to do, but are a bit disillusioned with its result. Goals that take a long time often involve a great deal of dreaming and visualizing about their culmination, and so it is typical for their achievement not to match the picture we've painted in our heads. No matter. The six is only the second in our series of three harmonies, and there is more to come if we can commit ourselves to harvesting now what we have paid for with our efforts.

Seven of Diamonds (Seven of Coins in Marseille)
Seven spelling wickedness...
Stone to keep all treasures...

The wickedness of stone lies less in its desire to take from others (though it can certainly be that) and more in its resistance to make even the smallest of concessions. This card often indicates that although circumstances have changed, the course of the project has not, and the plan is now ill-fitted for the world in which it is to come about. When we cling desperately to what we perceive as our only resource, our only means of getting where we mean to be, we overlook the many other paths that may take us there. Worse, we trample over many kind and helpful guides along the path with our curt and dismissive words. We have become too wrapped up in collecting our treasures to notice the people we are hurting along the way, and this will eventually spell ruin, for lasting achievement is only accomplished with the support of others. Perhaps we have cut some corners along the way or even dismissed some elements of self-care in order to achieve our goal. These little "cheats" we have relied on will soon come back to haunt us in full force unless we heed the warning and adopt a more flexible, more gentle approach.

Eight of Diamonds (Eight of Coins in Marseille)
Eight to take the reins...
Stone to keep all treasures...

Movement and change are less dignified in the suit of stone, and so we are faced with a conflict. The cart we pull behind us is heavy and overburdened with all of the treasures we have collected, and as a result, it is difficult to turn, its wheels dug deeply into the grooves of the road beneath us. And yet, turn we must. This is a time for revisiting even the most basic calculations we made when we first devised this plan and chose this route. If we cannot force the cart to turn, we risk being left behind, our achievements grinding to a halt in the sludge and knee-deep mud of this neglected road. On the other hand, if we are successful in our efforts to replot our trajectory, we can be assured of a carefully chosen and secure plan for success, since our suit is ever reliable and firm in its decisions.

Nine of Diamonds (Nine of Coins in Marseille)
Nine, a cornucopia...
Stone to keep all treasures...

Few cards are as favorable as the ninth iteration of stone. Our last harmony indicates blessings overflowing, for the treasures we have been harvesting over many long days have culminated not only in security, but in resplendency. After much toil and careful planning, there is now more than we dreamed possible. If the six represents the achievement of the goal, then the nine brings the exceeding of what we set out to accomplish. Looking back, the measures we once thought spelled our success are revealed to be meager and unworthy of us. We are more than we thought ourselves, and our sense of self-worth now swells in order to accommodate the new person we have become. This can be a joyful process, but it can be a painful one, too. The box in which we once placed ourselves is an ill fit, and we must reevaluate our expectations of ourselves, recognizing at last that *we* are the treasure we have been collecting all this time, and that our life is meant to be lived in the satisfaction of the joys and pleasures we once denied ourselves.

Ten of Diamonds (Ten of Coins in Marseille)
Ten, completion's crown...
Stone to keep all treasures...

Who will we be without our endless labor, without our worry, without our grueling effort spent collecting the treasures now that the work is done? The goal we set for ourselves is accomplished, and the time has come to move on to other things, but can we? The season asks us to put down our shovel and our hoe, to lay aside our gardening gloves and rest, to enjoy the fruits of our labor, but on this journey, we have allowed the garden to become such a part of us that we have difficulty imagining ourselves without it. The solution is this: we must help others tend their gardens, knowing that they will make mistakes, that we will have to bear witness to their various failures and stumbles along the way. The true harvest we have reaped is not the fruit itself, but the mastery of the process of growth, the journey that brought us there, and that knowledge can only be actualized if we are willing to share it with others who are in desperate need of help as they tend to gardens of their own.

Jack of Diamonds (Page of Coins in Marseille)
Jacks are ever learning...
Stone to keep all treasures...

Learning in the suit of stone is tedious and demanding, and our knave is drawn to this path by his meticulous, detail-oriented nature. He enjoys slow projects that are predictable and repetitive, and he appreciates stillness and quiet. Others may call him dull or remark that he is beating his head against a stone as he appears to make little progress towards his goals, but something within the knave tells him that he is exactly where he is meant to be. He is easily frustrated by unpredictability and chaos and sometimes struggles to understand the emotions of others, but those who connect with him will find a loyal friend who is humble and easily able to admit mistakes, never hesitating to learn from an error. In simplified cartomantic systems, this card is associated with Capricorn, the cardinal sign of earth, and with an aspect of the querent's own personality.

Queen of Diamonds (Queen of Coins in Marseille)
Queens are ever wise...
Stone to keep all treasures...

This aspect of our queen can be best understood as the embodiment of nurturing and steadiness. She understands that there is a season for all things and is well-suited to the task of bringing out the best in her subjects, looking beyond their immediate actions and circumstances in order to foster the potential within. She understands that every subject in her kingdom has a unique strength and power within them, and she views people themselves as her true treasures. Her expectations are high, but her generous nature means that she is always willing to help others rise to the occasion. She is annoyed, however, with those who undervalue themselves or fear commitment, turning a cold shoulder to the unfaithful and to those who lack resolve. Still, since love is the root of all wisdom, she is always able to forgive given enough time (and it may be quite a long time, given her nature). Minor setbacks and challenges have no power over her; she brushes off each challenge and recommits to the work before her anew, her stony eyes ever-focused on the far-away goal that may take years or decades to reach culmination. For her, it is no matter. Time will prove her right, and those she nurtures will find comfort in knowing that they are each precious and priceless at their core, and that all things will work out as they are meant to. In simplified cartomantic systems, this card is associated with Virgo, the mutable sign of earth, and with an aspect of the querent's own personality.

King of Diamonds (King of Coins in Marseille)
Kings seek to gain power…
Stone to keep all treasures…

If life is made up of the "haves" and the "have-nots," our king of stone is determined to be one of the "haves," regardless of the price or the consequences. Moreover, he is determined to rule over a prosperous kingdom, a nation of "winners" who set goals and achieve them, and as a result, he has no tolerance for what he perceives as failure on the part of anyone, including himself. Whereas the queen seeks to nurture others along the path of accrual and self-enrichment, helping them discover their self-worth, the king insults and bullies. He views failure as a personal weakness, and it is in this characteristic that he is most pitiable, for over the course of his life, he is sure to experience some failure or another, and his constitution is too brittle to withstand it. His self-worth snaps like a twig, and he spirals in self-loathing. He may turn to the queen or to the knave for reassurance in these moments, which they will give because they have kind hearts, but he will quickly forget the lesson. When others experience failure, he scolds them or abandons them, afraid that the lack of success may be contagious. Trapped in this cycle of egoism, he envies the sure-footed conviction of the queen, and deep down, he knows that he will never achieve its like. In simplified cartomantic systems, this card can represent Taurus, the fixed sign of earth, and an aspect of the querent's self.

Knight of Coins (Marseille)

The aggressive nature of the knight does little to complement the staying, lasting properties of the suit of stone. This character is eager and energized at the beginning of projects, but lacks the long-term planning to see them through, often abandoning his work in a half-formed state. His energy is electrifying to those around him, though, and he is able to instill much confidence and build attention around an idea with very little effort. If he leans into his skills of building energy and motivation, our knight can be a powerful asset in any project, but he will need to remind himself of long-term goals and to seek to more clearly embody the patient, steady properties of his suit in order to achieve fulfillment in his purpose.

Ace of Clubs (Ace of Rods in Marseille)
Ace to start the journey...
A crook to firmly guide...

As a suit, clubs bring ascension, elevation in status, and projects of a more creative and illustrious nature than those we see under diamonds. We are pulled along by the force of inspiration, and our principles may yet make us a leader, taking responsibility for the journeys of others who are impacted by our decisions, for good or ill. The journey in this suit is about the achievement of power and prestige, but whether this status will be used to serve others or dominate them ruthlessly is uncertain. The seed that sparks this journey, as enumerated in the first number of this suit, is the early spark of passion that moves us to seek the new. Under the influence of this card, we hunger to be more than we are, and we sense the stirrings of greatness somewhere within us, waiting to be unleashed. Perhaps in this vision, we see the possibility of freedom from those who have rendered us subservient in the past, and so we set off on our own now, to risk everything in the name of belonging solely to ourselves. In practical terms, this can represent the initiation of new endeavors designed to feed that fire within us, to branch out in some creative fashion, to throw caution to the wind and embark upon a journey of self-discovery. We may not have the accomplishments that we so long for yet, and there may be few who believe we can manage the trials to come, but we have confidence and passion on our side. Now is the time to believe in ourselves, to be our own champion, and to respond in the affirmative to invitations to make some wild change in our lives.

Two of Clubs (Two of Rods in Marseille)
Two to make a pair...
A crook to firmly guide...

The sharing of power is a complicated matter, and so the influence of the two is ill-suited to the nature of our suit of the crook. Here are tense relationships with uncomfortable power dynamics that may present themselves in a number of fashions. In partnerships, it may feel as if one party always has the upper-hand, or that grudges and debts are held over both, transforming every act and deed into a mere exchange of authority rather than a genuine expression of feeling. It could also be that one party consistently holds the upper hand in this relationship, making true equality impossible. Worse still, we could find ourselves with two parties who both consider themselves entitled to more than the other is willing to give, both imagining themselves to be the lord of their own kingdom, unable to honor each other in the way both feel they deserve. These need not be romantic relationships, merely exchanges of power. The solution in all cases lies in defining one's kingdom in specific and concrete terms and laying clear lines of territory. Both parties must accept that they cannot rule over anything and everything, but that they each have specific areas of skill and expertise, that they are each blessed with their own strengths and weaknesses. In the recognition of this, they can then seek out places where they complement one another, and so there is still hope of forming a harmonious alliance.

Three of Clubs (Three of Rods in Marseille)
Three, a sapling growing...
A crook to firmly guide...

The growth provided by our first harmony expresses itself in the suit of the crook as a kindled fire, somewhat tamed and shaped through discipline, but still hungry and vivacious in nature. Here we find the passionate young artist who imagines himself a visionary, even though he has only completed a handful of decent paintings. Drunk on early accomplishments, this can be a delicious place to languish, but the three ever wants to grow, and so we must make use of this drive and motivation to challenge ourselves. Now is the time to make the extra effort, to push ourselves beyond the limits in pursuit of our passions, for there are two more harmonies on the way on our journey through the suit of ascension, and there is much more to be seen, much more to learn and accomplish. We must remember that a fire, if it wants to survive, must continue to consume. It must stay hungry.

Four of Clubs (Four of Rods in Marseille)
Four, a stable chair...
A crook to firmly guide...

If the four is the most grounded and unmoving of the numbers, then it finds itself challenged by the suit of passion. Like the four's expression in the hearts suit, the tempestuous nature of the crook complicates the four's energy, yielding a few distinct possibilities in a reading. On the one hand, this may relate to the more lasting and permanent gifts of discipline over inspiration. While inspiration is fleeting, coming and going as it wills, discipline teaches us to commit to creating whether we feel inspired or no, to take full command of our passions in order to render them reliable when we will. On the other hand, the fire of this suit demands regular growth and change, and this is something the four cannot provide. We may feel creatively trapped or blocked, unable to accomplish the things that once came easy to us. This problem can be solved by breaking the confines of the box that constrains us, which is, in actuality, one of our own design. When we set expectations of ourselves based on what we have done in the past, we shrink and reduce ourselves, and so the key here is often to pursue our passions, to chase our muse without worrying about meeting any expectations at all. We can set ourselves free at any time by letting go of our preconceived notions of ourselves.

Five of Clubs (Five of Rods in Marseille)
Five to throw the carriage...
A crook to firmly guide...

As the first discord, the five is never a good thing per se, but in the suit of the crook, it is less disastrous—if approached from the right perspective. What passion wants most of all is to burn, consume, and satisfy its desires, and beckoned on by the five's chaotic and disruptive current, it will do so with wild abandon. But this is an evening of fun that goes a bit too far, a leap of faith taken without due consideration, an embrace of passion that we can be sure will create drama and strife later. The five cares not for the consequences of our actions, and the suit of the crook finds this exhilarating in the short term, but further down the road, we find disappointment, since we never intended to wreak ruin and chaos, only to fulfill the desire of our heart. Thankfully, clubs leave us less prone to moping and regret, so we are able to pick up the pieces and build anew, hopefully having learned a valuable lesson. The exhilaration we feel when letting go of worries and consequences must have its limits, otherwise, the fire spreads and consumes all of its fuel at once and is left with nothing to sate its hunger later.

Six of Clubs (Six of Rods in Marseille)
Six to gather grain...
A crook to firmly guide...

In a perfect state of balance and harmony, power acts in deep consideration of those impacted by our decisions, and our passions move us towards greater fulfillment and wholeness. Such are the blessings of this suit expressed in the six, the second harmony. No longer are we the young and impassioned, if presumptuous, creatives we once were. Now, our fire is brought into fair and careful negotiation with the forces around us, yielding reciprocity, an awareness that we do not act alone, but in coordination with many others and in the context of a complicated arena of powers. This can express itself as feeling a deep sense of alignment with the heart-rooted work we are engaged in, as participating in relationships of mutual benefit, and as shifts into positions of authority that feel as natural as our own skin because we are supported by those we lead. We may find a validating return on our previous investments of time and effort in the form of creative successes, accolades, or elevations in status. The sense of "flow" we experience in this state is rewarding and enriching, drawing on our deep ambitions in order to channel the fires of passion into something elegant and beneficial to the world around us. In order to maintain this harmony, we must remember that this celebrated status was not something we accomplished alone, but through the offerings and support of others, an ornate dance with many actors and movements, and we must endeavor to share the gifts that flow our way with those who need our help.

Seven of Clubs (Seven of Rods in Marseille)
Seven spelling wickedness...
A crook to firmly guide...

The seven is selfish. It desires to turn all things inward like a vacuum, devouring and destroying all around it in order to fill a hole inside that is, in reality, endless, a hunger that can never be sated, a pain that cannot be soothed. In this state of blind appetite, the club suit reveals its power-related qualities: ambitions that seek to harm other people, abuses of power, the twisting of our creative passions towards dark and harmful outlets. Perhaps we have grown too accustomed to having our way and have forgotten to consider the needs and feelings of others. In this case, we must loosen our grip on the power we hold; if it is harmonious, it will be returned to us in kind, validating our rightfulness in holding it and reminding us that balanced, healthy power is given and not taken. Depending on position, this may indicate a toxic power dynamic in the querent's life, someone or something that dominates us and saps our energy in order to destroy us. The solution here is to cut off the flow. We must cease feeding the fire that would only burn us and instead nourish ourselves with that energy, lest it take everything from us and leave us ruined. The core of this card lies in the perspective of seeing other people as twigs for kindling, as resources waiting to be consumed, and so we must remind ourselves that we are no better than those around us—but also no worse. We are equally deserving each of our fair share of fulfillment and power.

Eight of Clubs (Eight of Rods in Marseille)
Eight to take the reins...
A crook to firmly guide...

Since passion and ambition are thrilled by swift gains, this suit is well favored in the sign of movement and change, and so the eight of clubs is generally a positive card—with certain caveats. This card often signifies a swift ascension in society, powerful currents of inspiration moving us, and rushing, vigorous changes in power dynamics. The rules of the game have shifted in the middle of play, and suddenly, more of the board is up for grabs. We must look carefully at what may be new around us, at what elements we can discern at work that may not have been there before. Emboldened by our suit, this sudden change is not a mere invitation, but a demand. We must move with the current if we hope to continue our journey, embracing this new situation with vigor, for in this suit, movement is as natural as breathing, and we will likely see more than one pivot along the path we are treading. Rest is our enemy here, not because we don't deserve it, for we may be wearied by all of the commotion around us, but because if we hesitate at this turning of the wheel, we may find ourselves beneath it rather than riding above it, trampled in the mud and regretting that we missed our moment to shine.

Nine of Clubs (Nine of Rods in Marseille)
Nine, a cornucopia...
A crook to firmly guide...

Our final harmony ushers forth an abundance of rewards beyond what we set out to accomplish, which may include illustrious positions of authority being attained, celebrated creative successes, and in general, passions and ambitions being rewarded beyond our wildest dreams. These are almost always unexpected gains, and in this suit, which is driven by hunger and drive, the nine loses a bit of the luster it has in other suits, for our plate can suddenly seem a little too full. All of these gifts are rewarding, of course, but they are also demanding, and whether it is our dance card, our invitations to perform at events, or our positions of leadership, life can suddenly feel a little too full. We must remember that the offerings placed before us by the nine are simply that: offerings. We need not consume everything before us at this feast. All that is asked of us is that we consider ourselves worthy and continue being who we are, that we bask in this moment of utter accomplishment and trust ourselves to choose. This is, after all, the hidden lesson woven into the very fabric of power: that in its attainment, we find ourselves free to choose our own path at long last.

Ten of Clubs (Ten of Rods in Marseille)
Ten, completion's crown...
A crook to firmly guide...

We have chased our passion down many roads, some invigorating and others harrowing, and now we come to what appears to be an ending. The suit of the crook dislikes quiet and stillness, and so this can be a difficult moment, reflecting on the people we have been over time in pursuit of our ambitions and reconciling those characters with the sudden tranquility in which we find ourselves. We must let go of our hustle now (or at least allow it to slow), and we feel the fire of passion within us somewhat sated and satisfied, but it is a strange feeling. That which we set out to accomplish has been attained, but that goal burned within us for so long that we can still feel its ache like a phantom limb. The suit of the crook is always desirous of more, yet what more is there? People who sacrifice their health, their finances, and their social lives in order to attain their goals sometimes find that the end yields bitter fruit. Perhaps this ending does not taste as sweet as we imagined because we became too narrowly focused in our dogged pursuit, losing track of some other part of ourselves that was also hungering for its goals. At this juncture, we must learn to feed our own fire by moving on to other things and setting goals that will perhaps nourish some new parts of ourselves or contribute to the journeys of others. In truth, we will always be that passionate, vivacious person we always were, but now that we have acquired our share, we can redirect that energy, and we must, for life is too full and rich to reduce to the chasing of any one dream or passion. We are, each of us, many things at once, full of many different hungers, and we must search within for the spark that will initiate our next journey.

Jack of Clubs (Page of Rods in Marseille)
Jacks are ever learning...
A crook to firmly guide...

In order to learn the ways of passion and power, our knave must seek exposure to the ways of the world around him, and so he becomes an explorer, an adventurer of sorts, a student of the world and its people. He may not know yet where his own passions lie, but he knows that he will only discover them through sampling a short stint down as many of the paths before him as he is able, scouting out avenues for his ambitions to grow. This person is hungry for life itself and eager to taste freedom, and though he can seem directionless in his efforts, that in itself is part of his growth, for he must stretch himself in many directions before he can find his niche. There will be mistakes along the way, and he is sure to wander down roads that he later regrets, but if each path is treated as a lesson, then his fun-loving and free-spirited nature will land him on his feet. Simplified cartomantic systems associate this card with Aries, the cardinal sign of fire, and with an aspect of the querent's own personality.

Queen of Clubs (Queen of Rods in Marseille)
Queens are ever wise...
A crook to firmly guide...

The wisdom that is the heart of our queen expresses itself with magnanimity and charm in the suit of clubs. Our queen understands the ways of power, passion, and desire, and in her understanding, she treasures most that rare and transformative iteration of willpower: self-control. Though her ambitions may be raging within her, she is able to maintain a perfect poker face in dealings of power, knowing deep within that she will not fail. Even with turbulent passion stoking her on, she is smooth and careful, maintaining composure, biding her time and waiting for the perfect moment to sate her desires. She also understands the deeply felt desires of others, and she is able to charm her subjects into her service not through manipulation, but through honoring their distinct passions and giving them their fair share of what they desire in exchange for what she wants. People in her presence feel seen, quickened, and emboldened, inspired to reach for more, and her victories always feel deserved to those who witness them. Because of her utter control over herself and her ability to coach others towards their desires, she is in truth a sorceress, adept in the disciplines of wish fulfillment and the alignment of action with the heart's deepest, unspoken desires. Anything she sets out to do will inevitably succeed, and her success is always to the benefit of all, for she balances the tender heart of the knave with the terrible will of the king. Simplified cartomantic systems associate this card with Sagittarius, the mutable sign of fire, and with an aspect of the querent's personality.

King of Clubs (King of Rods in Marseille)
Kings seek to gain power...
A crook to firmly guide...

Our king of the crook imagines himself the perfect leader, knowing always what is best for his subjects, and driven by his passions, he seeks to shape his kingdom with a forceful hand, sculpting it into the vision that is so close he can taste it on his tongue. Yet, in valuing power over wisdom, he desires all for himself and none for others, and so he commands without listening, negotiates without compromising, and creates without perspective. He is unable to process any degree of criticism, which leaves his efforts flawed and ill-conceived. Maintaining his power requires constant effort since his subjects distrust his ambitions, and our poor king finds himself at the mercy of exhaustion and paranoia. Beneath his narcissism, he fears betrayal at all times and sees enemies everywhere. His lust for power and domination is untempered by self-control, so he is impatient when his commands are not immediately obeyed, falling into fits of rage and lashing out at those a wiser leader would treat as allies. If our king would simply heed the sound advice of others, he could still fulfill all of his desires, but he would also win the loyalty of his people. Simplified cartomantic systems associate this card with Leo, the fixed sign of fire, and with an aspect of the querent's personality.

Knight of Rods (Marseille)

The tempestuous knight of rods wishes to act the part of the hero, to swoop into the fray and seize glorious victory, to set his passion aflame like a bonfire. Unfortunately, his eagerness is not matched by his discipline, and so he often ends up inciting chaos by inserting himself into situations that have little to do with him, then vanishing when things go sour. He is drawn to conflict like a moth to the flame, and he is possessed of enormous sensual and sexual appetites. Despite his flaws, our knight's vivacious nature is alluring to others, and he is a panacea for those around him who feel stuck or bored in their circumstances. His courage allows him to throw caution to the wind and risk everything for the sake of his heart's desire. Perhaps if he can master the art of awakening passions in others, of emboldening and encouraging those who need him, he can find some usefulness, and at last feel that he is truly the hero he means to be.

The Diversity of Historic Cartomancy Systems

Cartomancy is not and has never been a dogmatic tradition or even a unified tradition. Models of cartomancy have always varied in their attribution of specific associations to individual cards, the basic structure of the card deck acting as a vessel for magical pneumonic devices of all varieties. This is nowhere more clear than in the folktale of the soldier and his cards. In this tale, a soldier attending a church service is seen to arrange playing cards before him instead of opening up the Bible. Since cards were associated with sin and devilry at the time, this was seen as an affront to religious authorities, and he was questioned for this action. He replies to his inquisitors with a litany of cartomantic associations with biblical events and figures, including the threes referring to the holy trinity, nines referring to the nine lepers cured by Christ, and queens referring to the Queen of Sheba. He goes on to associate the number of cards (52) with the number of weeks in a year, the number of markings on the cards (365) with the days in a year, and the numbers or classes (13) with the lunar months. This folktale teaches us that the simplicity of the playing card deck belies its abilities as a systemic tool for preserving complex patterns and oscillations of symbolism useful in both divination and magic.

In order to provide a glimpse of the diversity of cartomancy as a whole and draw these texts into conversation with one another, I'd like to summarize here some cartomantic systems preserved in our history. Although they differ in detail from the adapted cartomantic system I recommend in this book, they still provide a useful glimpse into how cartomancy has evolved over time. Learning how diverse and pluralistic approaches to cartomancy have always been, even in ages long past, frees us to explore what works for us as individual readers. As a cartomancer, there is really no such thing as being too "eclectic" or "non-traditional" because there exists no singular, organized tradition from which to depart.

The following correspondences published in Lucy and Daniel Thomas' (1920) *Kentucky Superstitions* may represent American practices in cartomancy distilled from the nineteenth century. Note the categorical structure used to identify persons with court cards based on age and complexion. Today, many readers find this type of system reductive and limiting, but this may have been related to similar methods of reading the court cards in tarot decks.

Ace of Clubs: An introduction.
Two of Clubs: New ventures in life.

Three of Clubs: A longer space of time (compared to the three of hearts).
Four of Clubs: A crowd, though smaller than the one in the hearts suit.
Five of Clubs: A ringing bell, a knock at the door, etc.
Six of Clubs: A carriage-ride or a motor.
Seven of Clubs: A journey across water.
Eight of Clubs: A business deal.
Nine of Clubs: Surety of good luck.
Ten of Clubs: A very long journey.
Jack of Clubs: A dark man.
Queen of Clubs: A dark woman.
King of Clubs: A dark, elderly man.
Ace of Hearts: A house or home.
Two of Hearts: A kiss.
Three of Hearts: A short space of time.
Four of Hearts: A pleasant crowd; dining and dancing.
Five of Hearts: A marriage.
Six of Hearts: Love.
Seven of Hearts: Jealousy.
Eight of Hearts: Many love affairs.
Nine of Hearts: Getting one's wish.
Ten of Hearts: The pleasures of love.
Jack of Hearts: A blonde young man.

Queen of Hearts: A blonde young woman.
King of Hearts: A gray, elderly man.

Ace of Diamonds: A letter.
Two of Diamonds: Very good luck.
Three of Diamonds: Three pieces of good fortune together.
Four of Diamonds: A pleasant crowd, though less so than in the hearts suit.
Five of Diamonds: A diamond ring.
Six of Diamonds: Money.
Seven of Diamonds: A conversation.
Eight of Diamonds: More money than the six of diamonds.
Nine of Diamonds: Disappointment.
Ten of Diamonds: More money than the eight of diamonds.
Jack of Diamonds: A very blonde young man.
Queen of Diamonds: A very blonde woman.
King of Diamonds: A very blond, elderly man.

Ace of Spades: A strange bed.
Two of Spades: Trouble, a lie, words of anger.
Three of Spades: A long period of time.
Four of Spades: An accident or sorrow that draws a crowd.

Five of Spades: Sickness.
Six of Spades: A funeral.
Seven of Spades: Tears.
Eight of Spades: A strong drink.
Nine of Spades: Disaster; the worst card in the deck.
Ten of Spades: A loss, though not necessarily as extreme as the other tens.
Jack of Spades: A very dark young man.
Queen of Spades: A very dark woman
King of Spades: A very dark elderly man.

***

The Spaewife or Universal Fortune-Teller (1827) provides lengthy attributions to the cards in the form of a series of poems ascribed to the eight, nine, ten, jack, queen, and king of each suit. Many of these poems are disturbing in their portrayal of women's fates at the time it was published, which were largely dictated by marriage. Modern cartomancy avoids gender binaries and heterosexist assumptions in order to draw inclusive wisdom that isn't poisoned by misogyny. Paraphrased here for the sake of brevity, these correspondences are as follows.

Eight of Hearts: If a woman, a sign of heavy drinking late in life and an amorous disposition; if a man, a sign of a large family and many duties.
Nine of Hearts: If a woman, travel by carriage; if a man, shallowness.
Ten of Hearts: If a woman, beauty, grace, and many children; if a man, no less than ten children, though he may regret having them.
Jack of Hearts: If a woman, a rascal or marriage to an elderly man; if a man, falling in love with a vixen.
Queen of Hearts: If a woman, many blessings and good fortune; if a man, enjoying the company of many women, but also regret.
King of Hearts: If a woman, lack of chastity and eventual widowhood; if a man, poverty and an unfaithful lover.

Eight of Spades: If a woman, wasting time with useless men; if a man, rogues operating around him.
Nine of Spades: If a woman, an old maid; if a man, bliss.
Ten of Spades: If a woman, a happy bride; if a man, a happy husband.
Jack of Spades: If a woman, ill news; if a man,

marriage to a cruel woman.

Queen of Spades: If a woman, elegance and grace; if a man, crudeness and an unhappy life.

King of Spades: If a woman, rejection from high society; if a man, acceptance in high society and a life of altruism.

Eight of Diamonds: If a woman, life as an old maid; if a man, a happy rural life.

Nine of Diamonds: If a woman, unhappiness and discontentment with one's circumstances, no matter how comfortable; if a man, disloyalty, disgrace, and death without an heir.

Ten of Diamonds: If a woman, peace and plenty, as well as ten children. An early grave if twins are born; if a man, a life-long bachelor.

Jack of Diamonds: If a woman, preoccupation with fools and knaves; if a man, a wasted youth.

Queen of Diamonds: If a woman and a widow, marriage again; if a man and married, a cheating spouse.

King of Diamonds: If a woman, marriage to a tyrant; if a man, favor among royalty and hatred from lower ranks.

Eight of Clubs: If a woman, a petty, selfish person;

if a man, a liar and a thief.
Nine of Clubs: If a woman, tragedy, disaster, misfortune; if a man, a hated harasser of women.
Ten of Clubs: If a woman, grief at the death of a loved one; if a man, the same.
Jack of Clubs: If a woman, love with a dumb brute; if a man, a liar.
Queen of Clubs: If a woman, premarital relations resulting in a child; if a man, the same.
King of Clubs: If a woman, good fortune and a loving husband; if a man, many friends.

***

Mother Bunch's Golden Fortune-teller (1857) introduces two systems of cartomancy. The first concerns only matters of love and utilizes only the hearts suit. These limited instructions provide something more akin to a parlor game than a full reading. The second of these is more comprehensive and provides more detailed explanations of card meanings. Most of the attributions here concern prospects of marriage and family life that would have been of interest to young women at the time.

Ace of Hearts: Feasting and pleasure.
Two of Hearts: Extraordinary success and good fortune.
Three of Hearts: Suffering resulting from imprudent choices.
Four of Hearts: A marriage late in life.
Five of Hearts: A wavering, unsteady, and unattached disposition.
Six of Hearts: A generous, open, and credulous disposition.
Seven of Hearts: A fickle and unfaithful disposition, addicted to vice.
Eight of Hearts: Drinking and feasting.
Nine of Hearts: Wealth, grandeur, and high esteem.
Ten of Hearts: Good nature and numerous children.
Jack of Hearts: Dearest friend or nearest relation (can be of either sex).
Queen of Hearts: A woman of fair complexion, faithful and affectionate.
King of Hearts: A good-natured man who can sometimes be rash and passionate.

Ace of Clubs: Great wealth, prosperity, and tranquility of mind.

Two of Clubs: Opposition to current endeavors.
Three of Clubs: Thrice married, each time to a wealthy person.
Four of Clubs: Inconstancy for the sake of money.
Five of Clubs: A marriage that will mend circumstances.
Six of Clubs: A lucrative partnership; well-behaved children.
Seven of Clubs: Fortune and bliss; trouble from the opposite sex.
Eight of Clubs: Greed and unhappiness from it.
Nine of Clubs: Hard-headedness; loss of friends.
Ten of Clubs: Unexpected riches and the loss of a friend.
Jack of Clubs: A true and loyal friend.
Queen of Clubs: A woman of a tender, mild, and amorous disposition.
King of Clubs: A man who is upright, affectionate, humane, and faithful.

Ace of Spades: Love, whether lawful or unlawful, or death.
Two of Spades: A coffin.
Three of Spades: A fortunate marriage to a person who turns out to be inconstant.

Four of Spades: Speedy sickness; friends injuring your fortune.
Five of Spades: Good luck in the choice of a companion; a sullen temperament.
Six of Spades: Mediocrity of fortune and uncertainty in undertakings.
Seven of Spades: Death of a valued friend.
Eight of Spades: Opposition from friends.
Nine of Spades: Disaster; worst card in the deck.
Ten of Spades: Ill tidings.
Jack of Spades: An unreliable person.
Queen of Spades: A corrupted person.
King of Spades: A successful, ambitious man.

Ace of Diamonds: A letter.
Two of Diamonds: An early love without family approval.
Three of Diamonds: Disagreements, quarrels, law-suits, and unhappy marriages.
Four of Diamonds: Marriage to an inconstant person.
Five of Diamonds: Good children.
Six of Diamonds: Premature widowhood; a second marriage that is worse.
Seven of Diamonds: Infidelity.
Eight of Diamonds: A person disinclined towards

marriage.
Nine of Diamonds: A constantly discontented person.
Ten of Diamonds: A partner from the country; wealth and many children.
Jack of Diamonds: A stubborn man who dislikes being disagreed with.
Queen of Diamonds: A woman fond of company and not overly virtuous.
King of Diamonds: An angry, vengeful man.

***

The History of Playing Cards with Anecdotes of Their Use in Conjuring (1865) includes a very succinct log of popular meanings utilized by "card-cutters" at the time. These bear some similarity to those provided in *Kentucky Superstitions* and may share some of the same origin, though with later adaptations.

Ace of Diamonds: A wedding ring.
Two of Diamonds: A clandestine engagement.
Three of Diamonds: Domestic quarrels; trouble; unhappiness.
Four of Diamonds: An unfaithful friend; a secret

betrayed.
Five of Diamonds: Unexpected, though generally good news.
Six of Diamonds: Early marriage, succeeded by widowhood.
Seven of Diamonds: Satire; scandal.
Eight of Diamonds: A happy marriage, though perhaps late in life.
Nine of Diamonds: A roving disposition; adventure in foreign lands.
Ten of Diamonds: Wealth; honorable success in business.
Jack of Diamonds: A selfish and deceitful friend.
Queen of Diamonds: A person fond of gaiety.
King of Diamonds: A person quick to anger, but easily appeased.

Ace of Spades: Sickness and death.
Two of Spades: A removal.
Three of Spades: Tears; a journey by land.
Four of Spades: Sickness.
Five of Spades: Great danger from a bad temper.
Six of Spades: A child.
Seven of Spades: The death of a relative; unexpected poverty.
Eight of Spades: Danger from imprudence.

Nine of Spades: Grief; ruin; sickness; death.
Ten of Spades: Disgrace; crime; imprisonment; execution.
Jack of Spades: A lawyer; a person to be avoided.
Queen of Spades: A malicious and vengeful person.
King of Spades: An overly ambitious person.

Ace of Hearts: A querent's home.
Two of Hearts: Success in life and a happy marriage.
Three of Hearts: Poverty, shame, and sorrow.
Four of Hearts: Domestic trouble caused by jealousy.
Five of Hearts: A gift.
Six of Hearts: Honorable courtship.
Seven of Hearts: Good friends.
Eight of Hearts: Fine things and invitations to high society events.
Nine of Hearts: Wealth and good position in society.
Ten of Hearts: Health, happiness, and many children.
Jack of Hearts: A sincere friend.
Queen of Hearts: A model of sincere affection, devotion, and prudence.

King of Hearts: A person slow to anger, but once upset, difficult to appease.

Ace of Clubs: A letter.
Two of Clubs: Disappointment; vexation.
Three of Clubs: Quarrels; being married more than once; three years, weeks, months or days.
Four of Clubs: Misfortune resulting from inconstancy.
Five of Clubs: A happy, though not wealthy marriage.
Six of Clubs: Competence by honorable industry.
Seven of Clubs: A prison; danger from the opposite sex.
Eight of Clubs: Danger from covetousness.
Nine of Clubs: Danger from drunkenness.
Ten of Clubs: Unexpected wealth from the death of a relative.
Jack of Clubs: A sincere friend, but with a touchy temper.
Queen of Clubs: An agreeable, genteel, and witty person.
King of Clubs: An honorable, true, and affectionate person.

***

Overall, we see the wild variety that has always been a part of cartomancy. One reader may have interpreted the nine of clubs as a sign of drunkenness, while another would read this card as a sign of excellent luck to come. The three of hearts could be read as an indication of a period of time relating to a circumstance signaled by some nearby card or as a sign of misfortune, depending on the reader's approach.

While we cannot ignore the reality of disagreement and divergence among these older models, we must recognize that certain patterns emerge. Among these, the most clear is the nature of suit, with hearts frequently concerning love and relationships, clubs more often indicating power and ambitions, diamonds with a tendency to suggest fortune (or lack thereof), and spades more often than other suits heralding especially dark and troublesome fates. Modern systems, including the one preserved in our guiding rhyme, "The Devil's Picture-Book," condense and incorporate this wisdom, distilling it down to a concentrated essence that still leaves the individual practitioner room to adapt.

By letting go of the illusion of a universal

cartomantic system, we are free to explore and adapt, and this impulse, in and of itself, is not a departure, but an integral part of the cartomantic tradition we have inherited. Exploration and adaptation, alongside our intuition, are keys to arriving at an effective form of cartomancy that works for us as individual readers.

Even at the heart of what we call "traditional" craft, our work often involves moving forward with the spirit of the art, while allowing its minutiae to evolve. While our modern approach draws on general (though, admittedly, imperfect) trends sourced in these models of the past, especially in terms of understanding the currents of suit and number, we cannot allow ourselves to be held prisoner by inventions devised to serve people living in a different age, a different culture, and a vastly different context than the one we experience. We must accept our inheritance of craft, grasping gently its heart of wisdom with a willingness to adapt and evolve it, pursuing our own position in its long and diverse lineage, which has, in truth, never been a fixed and immovable thing.

Reflecting on the Marseille Trumps

All of the principles, spreads, and techniques discussed in this work are transferable to the unillustrated minor cards in the Marseille tarot tradition. Hearts change into cups, clubs into batons, spades into swords, and diamonds into coins. The lack of illustrations, a chief difference between older tarot decks and newer ones based on Arthur Edward Waite's system, becomes not a hindrance, but a strength, allowing the reader to intuit, analyze, and discern convergences of suit and number in a freer and less prescriptive method of reading.

Before de Gebelin, Levi, and Waite repositioned tarot as a tool of ceremonial and qabalistic magic (sometimes spelled *magick* in the style of Aleister Crowley), older decks with unillustrated minor cards were utilized in divination and folk magic with more traditional, common-sense roots, so it is worth exploring the possibilities of this deck in association with the folk witchcraft revival taking place today (Ben-Dov, 2017).

The most striking, meaningful difference between playing cards and Marseille tarot decks lie in the trump cards, a separate grouping of twenty-two illustrated cards. Unlike the minors, these cards are illustrated lusciously, and we must now begin to consider where these images are leading us, what structure guides the form they take, and how we shall use and employ them in the context of reading and conjuring.

The trump cards (sometimes referred to as the "major arcana") are heavy in symbolic imagery derived from a variety of sources, including medieval mystery plays, the danse macabre motif, european folklore, ancient pagan virtues, astrology, greek mythology, and biblical texts and interpretations (Huson, 2004; Ben-Dov, 2017). While we do not know who illustrated the first tarot deck, we can surmise that the artist drew on these sources (consciously or unconsciously) in order to craft the basis of a card game with an air of wit, playfulness, and mystery. More importantly, whether intentional or not, these cards have so impressed themselves upon our collective memory that they have taken on a life of their own and now offer a door to much spiritual mystery.

Rather than relying upon tables of qabalistic correspondences and assigned keywords, the folk witch method of reading the Marseille tarot involves observing what is actually present in the imagery of the cards as printed in earlier centuries, using common sense to discern the theme and careful pattern analysis to understand the structure that guides them.

In the Star, for example, we have a naked

woman pouring water into a pool and onto the earth in a beautiful night-time scene. We might read this card as representing freedom from convention (being naked in the wilderness), generosity (pouring water), appreciation for beauty (the landscape and the beautiful woman), or vulnerability (again, being unclothed in the wild), depending on its position in a spread and the intuition of the reader.

A topic rarely addressed in tarot writing is the observation of inherent patterns in the trumps. Rather than seeking to impose an external pattern or structure in the manner of qabalistic tarot studies, we can look closely at what is actually in the deck to discern two distinct structures at work.

On the one hand, the progression of the cards has a broadening scope, beginning quite small and localized with the Fool (technically number zero), who is depicted as a mad vagabond roaming the wilderness, at the mercy of the dog chasing and biting him, and increasing until we at last reach the World, the most all-encompassing trump. Each card is meant to be read as more powerful and influential than the one before it, and we, as players (or in our case, cartomancers), are left to wonder where we stand in this grand design. This ever-expanding movement that we witness through the trump suit echoes the cosmologies of early modern period, which imagined the universe as a series of spheres reaching outward, with earth and the human self placed at its center. While we understand today that the universe is vast and we are by no means its center or reason for existing, this view is ingrained in the structure of the Marseille tarot, and it still has something to offer us today. As a useful exercise, consider setting the trumps out before you in order, one at a time, and considering how and why this sequence exists. Why, for instance, might the Star have been considered beyond the influence of the Tower? Why is the humble Hermit outside of the influence of Justice?

While the vast forces depicted in the trump sequence, such as the Sun and Moon and even Death itself, may naturally make us feel small as they dwarf the human figures in the cards, we must remember what the trumps ultimately are: cards. We are meant to hold them, to shuffle them, to manipulate them, to play with them like toys, and in these actions, we are empowered in both game and ritual. We are like the early humans who began developing the art of language, wielding sign and symbol that feel too grand and potent for us, but are nonetheless tools at our disposal. We are, when wielding the trumps, like gods ourselves, moving the forces of the universe about in our hands, and so it is no wonder that this inherently magical act is part of the reason our cards were associated with sorcery and witchcraft from very early in their development.

Building upon this concept of expansive movement through the trump sequence, we can also witness certain synergies. Many of the three cards that appear in a sequence contain a kind of riddle to do with how two distinct forces (the first and third) come together to influence another (the second). For example, the Hanged Man falls directly between Strength and Death in the trump ordering. (This original order was later manipulated by Waite in his deck in order to suit his idiosyncratic take on these cards.) What might this original order mean? In Strength, we see a figure prying open the mouth of a ferocious lion, uninhibited by fear and unravaged by the beast. In Death, we witness the familiar version of the reaper born of the danse macabre tradition of illustrations: a skeleton gleefully hacking away with his scythe. Our Hanged Man, who falls in the middle, is the victim of "baffling," a form of punishment in olden days in which the victim was hung upside down until he expired, presumably from brain hemorrhaging. If Strength suggests power over ferocious forces, what do we become when we attempt to wield power over the unmovable, when we refuse to accept the truth of Death as a natural power in the world that cannot be conquered? It would be wise for us to examine the trump sequence in pairs of three in order to study the logic of previous centuries and what it may have to teach us today.

The other key structure we can discern from analyzing the trump sequence is a kind of pairing and reflecting that seems to be quite intentional. Certain cards mirror one another in ways that transcend mere coincidence, and by exploring these pairs, we can better understand the imagery in the cards and their significance. Here, then, are some observable pairings for the reader's own exploration and experimentation.

The Empress and The Emperor

It was long the understanding of previous ages that men and women ruled over different spheres in life, and most modern Marseille readers disregard the misogyny of this assumption and focus instead on those spheres themselves, which may apply to both men and women based on personality rather than gender. While the Emperor rules over the external affairs of his many territories, expanding and reinforcing his power over many kingdoms, the Empress' power is within the palace and the court. It is she who moves the players about within the inner sphere of power, and in truth, it is she who most influences the Emperor himself, directing his attention to those projects that suit her fancy. These two approach rulership in different ways and can be said to depict different types and structures of power within which we operate under our various laws and various countries.

The Popess and The Pope

Much like the Empress and Emperor, the Popess and Pope depict different types of authority that exist beyond the scope of laws. These are the authorities of belief, of morals and conventions and societal expectations. The Pope is a very clear figure representing the head of the church, a power to which most of Europe would bow at different points in time, but the Popess is more enigmatic. She is, in fact, a reference to Pope Joan, a folkloric figure who, in the tales, ascended to the level of Pope without anyone knowing she was a woman until she finally gave birth, shocking witnesses to the event. Our Popess can be said to signify the power of belief held inwardly, of the ethics, values, and spiritual laws we develop within ourselves and for ourselves. She can also indicate a sense of righteousness within us even when external forces would disagree.

The Devil and The Lovers

At first glance, the Devil and the Lovers appear to mirror each other not in terms of content, but in terms of composition: a winged figure positioned over a gathering of humans. In the case of the Lovers, we have a person torn between two sweethearts with a cupid figure looming above, but in the case of the Devil, we have instead demonic figures presided over by the king of hell himself. While later versions of the Lovers seem to allude to Adam and Eve, this image is clearly based instead in a moment of indecision, of feeling pulled romantically in more than one direction, perhaps seeing beauty and pleasure everywhere and thus being unable or unwilling to commit ourselves anywhere. The Devil, on the other hand, is decisive: *you are both mine*, he says to the lovers who are now demons. The Devil's body in the Marseille trump is worth dissecting here briefly, for it is composed of various animal and monster parts. While the Devil represents those things we fear, he also possesses a potency and a certainty that the Lovers card seems to lack.

The Sun and The Moon

While probably the most obvious pairing in the trump sequence, this reflective pair of astral bodies is still worth dissecting, for these figures are enduring in myth and folklore, and they will never run out of lessons for us. While the Sun hovers over a twin pair of youths below, the Moon perches over a pair of wolves with a crustacean emerging from the pool. In previous ages, it was commonly believed that the moon ruled over dreams and madness, which transformed humans into beasts, while the sun was seen as orderly and healthful, providing the cycles necessary to agriculture.

Today, we know better, of course: both the cycles of the sun and the moon are necessary to the balance of the natural world. Without the Moon, we are insomniacs, either literally or figuratively, unable to sleep or unable to dream and envision. Without the Sun, we are unable to see things clearly in days' light, lost in mists and fog and illusion, and perhaps in our own imaginings of what might be lingering in the dark.

Death and The Fool

This pairing is less obvious from an image analysis perspective, but the naming and ordering devices at work in the trump sequence make it clearer. Death is the only card that is not given a name, and the Fool is the only card not given a number. Both are treated by special rules in the trump sequence, and so we must consider them together and try to discern what sets them apart. The Fool is perhaps the most vulnerable character; even his clothing is falling apart as he stumbles through the wilds, chased and harried by a dog. The Italian name for this card, "Il Matto," signifies both a beggar and an insane person. In many folktales, it is the wandering beggar who secretly possesses great wisdom and power, but on a literal level, this figure is quite pitiful. Death, on the other hand, is invulnerable and permanent. It is a deep truth of the universe that all things must die in their time. In these two, we see the human actor, vulnerable and naked as he is, and the arena of law in which he must act, the self alongside the final truth that gives meaning and purpose to the choices we make. Without the truth of Death, who are we? Ironically, it is in the fact that our time is limited that we find motivation and drive to make the journey in the first place. It is only in the foreknowledge of our end that we can truly live and appreciate living.

Justice and Temperance

Both of these principles can be readily identified as "cardinal virtues" that the church adopted from the classical pagan world. These are meant to be understood as principles to live by, qualities to foster in oneself and in those around us, and deep values of a harmonious society. While Justice refers to a careful balance of action in consideration of others, Temperance signifies a balance held within the self. These are, in truth, the same principle interpreted through the lenses of the internal and the external. When acting with Justice, we act with consideration of the needs of others, paying our debts and abiding by laws so as not to inhibit the necessary freedoms of others as we seek those things that matter to us. When acting with Temperance, we exercise self-restraint when engaging in our pleasures and caution when straining ourselves, taking all things in moderation so as not to spoil the pleasures of life with slovenly excess or poison the disciplines we enjoy with unnecessary suffering.

Strength and The Juggler

These two figures, on a visual level, appear to be wearing the same hat in the Marseille illustrations, but on deeper analysis, we find many more meaningful parallels between them. In the renaissance mind, there was little distinction made between the conjurer and the stage magician; both were seen as mysterious trickster figures in popular literature, and the lines were frequently blurred between them because they were considered to have power over the minds of others, to manipulate perception in order to achieve their ends. Similarly, the figure depicted in Strength wields power over those brutal forces in life that would otherwise destroy us, in this case shown as a beast. Again, as in the Sun and Moon cards, we see a value statement regarding the human and animal worlds. To wield power over the beast would have been considered by our ancestors a sign of strength, but to wield power over human minds would have been a violation of reason. No matter. In these two cards, we can simply interpret two iterations of control pushed in different directions.

Judgment and The Star

Here, we find two signs of divine favor, though of two very different varieties. In ancient times, the morning star was recognized as Venus, but also associated with Lucifer, the light-chaser, who was later synergized mythologically as an aspect of the Devil. Even later, the star was associated with the birth of Christ and the promise of the salvation of the world. In previous ages, though, the morning star was simply a sign of hope, of the coming of dawn even while darkness surrounds us, and the figure in this card is bathing naked, pouring out water upon the earth, unafraid to be vulnerable and alone in the night. Hope in this card seems to be a nourishing force, but we must take it without sign or token that our dreams will ever come about. We have only the symbol of the star to guide us through the night. Judgment, on the other hand, depicts the revival of faithful Christians from their graves with the second coming as the angel of the apocalypse sounds its trumpet. In this card, we are offered not only hope, but promise. We are told in no uncertain terms that all debts will be settled and rewards given, but the result is only happy for those willing to submit completely to the authority that carries this banner.

The Chariot and The Hanged Man

These two cards speak to one another not for their similarities, but because they could not be more different in nature. The Chariot depicts a victorious roman returning from battle in a sort of ceremonial festival of homecoming that we know was performed in the ancient world. The Hanged Man, on the other hand, conveys humiliation, punishment, and social ostracization. It is worth noting that "baffling," the form of upside-down hanging we see here, was a sentence carried out for those labeled as traitors, perhaps inflicted as a kind of poetic justice upon those whose loyalties were perceived to as inverted. However, we all know that societal perception is not always accurate or objective, and those who are celebrated the loudest are sometimes the worst traitors of all. These cards do not depict the actual deeds or characters of the two figures, only the public response: either complete adoration or utter loathing.

The Tower and The Hermit

There are two roots of the imagery in the Tower, and both can be justified with sources and historicity. Some argue that the Tower is based on the Tower of Babel, and that the ruin we see inflicted upon the tower is the result of an angry god punishing humans for advancing too far in their architecture, their science, their magics, and in short, in civilization as a whole. Others argue that the source of this imagery is rooted in the myth of the harrowing of hell, which is the journey said to be taken by Christ after his crucifixion in order to lead all of the good and benevolent soles out of one of hell's towers and into heaven. This card is complex, but its root is a breaking and shattering of things in order to make room for something new that must come about. The Hermit, meanwhile, seeks after the breakage of the society's shackles and the dissolution of the self, to unravel the mysteries of his own soul in order to find salvation within. We can also view this pair as a commentary on the ruin of overreaching, of imagining oneself to be more important than we may actually be, and the price of self-impoverishment and heavy-handed forms of modesty and discipline, which leave us isolated and deprived of all comforts.

The Wheel of Fortune and The World

Both of these cards depict a version of Fortuna, goddess of Fortune, who is said to balance on a great globe, frequently depicted with a ship's wheel as her emblem. In metaphysical terms, we can understand these two as time or circumstance (the Wheel) and space or physicality (the World), and from that perspective, it is only in the rotations and permutations of these two that all human affairs exist. In readings, though, the Wheel tells us that something has changed, for its imagery is an old world trope depicting persons of various positions in society rotating as it turns. The king appears to be at the top of the wheel for now, but it is sure to turn, so we cannot assume he will be there forever. Similarly, the World is an orb upon which Fortuna treads, turning it this way and that, the lesson of which seems to be that we are, ultimately, small and insignificant in terms of the greater picture.

Other, sometimes imperfect pairings exist outside of these arrangements, and they are still worth considering in the study of the trumps. The Devil and The Star, for instance, seem rooted in two streams of discourse surrounding the figure of Lucifer as both the morning star and the ruler of hell. The fact that these two cards find the Tower between them can be no mere coincidence. Likewise, Judgment and the Lovers bear a striking resemblance in terms of visual composition, and so we must consider what this comment means, how the service of otherworldly powers and the afterlife is affected or interrupted by the pursuit of amorous pleasures in this life.

Pairs not detailed here seem to contain riddles that players of card games hundreds of years in the past may have understood more keenly than we are capable of grasping today. The cartomancer would be wise to sit with observable pairings for exercises in reflection and close observation of the imagery they contain. All cartomancy, both tarot-based and playing card-based, has roots in the practice of reflective thought. From this basic practice of quietly observing patterns and meaning, we derive our great wealth of divinatory and magical practice.

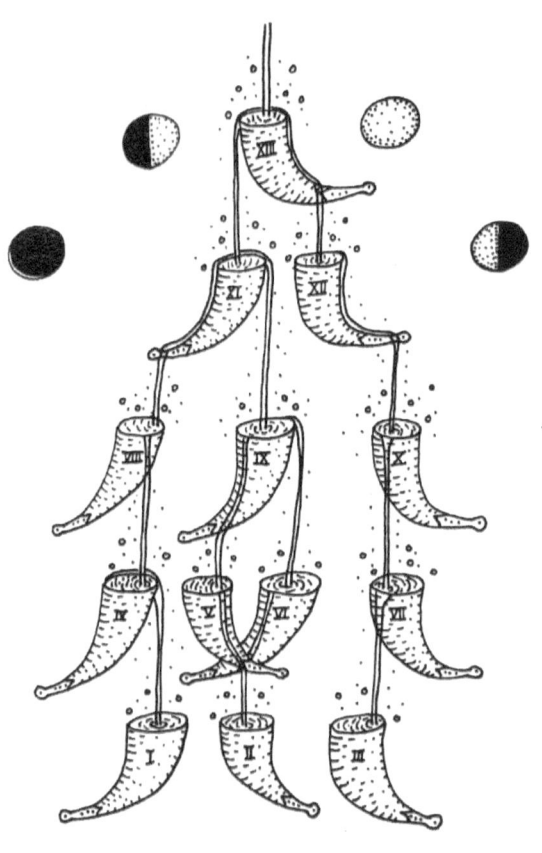

Reading the Cards

When it comes to interpreting and reading the cards, many cartomancers must go through a period of unlearning. In other learnable skills, we are taught to use a linear approach. Do this, then do that, and you will have accomplished the task. In modern cartomancy, this is not the case. We cannot say for certain that a card in a particular position will always indicate any one circumstance. Even if we could, what would be the point? What we're after isn't a soulless, paint-by-numbers approach to card reading. After all, it is the reader who interprets and weaves the threads together, not a table of assigned keywords and prescriptive associations.

Instead, we must learn to see a landscape in a spread and to observe layers of patterns. For example, we may begin by teasing out numbers and suits that appear most frequently. What might this pattern mean? Perhaps one suit is completely absent from the spread. What might this absence be telling us? If certain cards with a shared number or suit are touching, perhaps this indicates a relationship between these forces. Although spreads can tell us how to approach a particular card, they cannot take the place of the reader. No two readers are the same, but a card reading is only performed by one reader. Just like the cards that are selected by fate, that reader is *meant* to interpret, to see. Doubt is useless to the cartomancer. Intuition and conviction are paramount.

Many querents come to readers seeking to know the future. Whether this is possible or ethical is a matter of debate among cartomancers. Here, I'll offer my perspective, but keep in mind that it is far from gospel. When we read the cards, we engage in the interpretation of patterns, and sometimes these patterns can form a kind of trajectory. It's a little like predicting the trajectory of a storm. We can offer guidance to the querent in terms of observable patterns, where those might lead, and how to break them, but we cannot truly predict with complete certainty how things will turn out in the end. Because of my perspective on this issue, I try to be careful to explain to the querent that I offer advisory readings, not predictive ones. Ultimately, my opinion is that having knowledge of an unavoidable future just isn't as useful as having real guidance to improve one's life in the present.

It may be desirable to develop a personal ritual to use before reading the cards. Most readers like to shuffle the cards briefly and may ask the querent to shuffle or "cut the deck" by dividing it in half at a random position and putting the deck back together. Getting the cards in the querent's hands, even for a moment, is often thought to forge a stronger connection between the cards and the querent, and I happen to believe there is something to this.

Most frequently, however, the querent is asked to choose a card to represent themselves, often called a "significator." This is typically one of the court cards, though the options for allowing a querent to choose a significator are as endless as the reader's creativity, and utilizing more than one option is certainly recommended when offering online readings. In choosing their significator (irrespective of gender for reasons previously stated), the querent reveals the dominant traits driving the question at hand. If the querent, for example, asks a question about love but chooses the Queen of Spades as his significator, we can quickly discern a person whose character is seasoned by knowledge of life's more difficult challenges. For this person, love is perhaps a more difficult matter to understand than it might be for the Queen of Hearts. On the other hand, if the heart's desire and the significator seem well-aligned, this often indicates that the querent has selected a significator representing qualities they *wish* to embody. This need not rattle the reader's approach, though, since knowing who a querent desires to become is just as informative and contextualizing, revealing via negation what they perceive as their flaws or shortcomings.

Perhaps most crucially, the reader should fully understand and claim the power they have when delivering a reading. The words we choose and the way we deliver them are not mere parlor tricks, but are impactful and potent to our querents. I often describe the work of divination as a form of spiritual medicine. This should come as no surprise, since we, ultimately, are participating in the meaningful work of restoring balance. Why else should all of our methods of pattern discernment focus on relationships between cards, absent cards, and dominant cards? Of ratios of suit and color? Of mirroring across lines of a spread? All of our methods of pattern discernment come down to this: what is out of balance here in this spread, and what would it look like for that balance to be restored? This is the medicine.

For the sake of flow and practicality, the reader should decide in advance whether the reading will take the form of a predetermined spread, and if so, whether it will utilize a single card, two cards, three cards, five cards, nine cards, or sixteen cards. Each of these spreads has its strengths, and so we will explore each individually. For the sake of cohesion, these examples will utilize the playing card suits, but remember that these translate readily into Marseille tarot suits since they evolved historically from the same source (hearts becoming cups, clubs becoming rods, spades becoming swords, and diamonds becoming coins).

The Single-Card Spread

The single card is read as a moment in a larger progression through the particular suit. For example, if the querent draws the five of hearts, they are moving away from the four of hearts. They might be asked to release stable relationships of the past. They are moving towards the six of hearts, which could indicate a reunion. In order to move forward, the querent must embrace the emotional destabilization of the five. Note that each suit is read as a cycle, the king being followed by a return to the ace.

Possible reading: *Let go of neediness and insecurity (4 of H). Holding on too tight will not keep near the thing you desire. Embracing the unknown in the present (5 of H) will yield greater fruits (6 of H) than you can currently imagine.*

The Two-Card Spread

This spread is useful for readings concerning relationships. Whether the two cards are harmonious can indicate the nature of the trajectory. Decide in advance which card (left or right) will represent the querent and which card will represent the other party. The nature of the cards that turn up can be read as key motivations behind the two actors in this situation.

Possible reading: *You want an adventure, to face challenges head-on, to learn and grow in new directions (5 of C). He wants to change his financial situation for the better (8 of D). Encourage him to take wise risks. Your willingness to go on this journey with him will bring you closer together.*

The Three-Card Spread

This is a very common-sense spread. The card on the left is read as the releasing current, indicating that which is departing and must be released in order to move forward. The card on the right is read as the embracing current, representing something that must be accepted or embodied. The center card is a resource or strength at the querent's disposal, something to help with the challenge of this transition.

Possible reading: *The suffering haunting you* (7 of S) *is cyclical; it wants to haunt your future as well* (9 of S), *but it is more punishment than you deserve. You'll need to rely on a loved one* (2 of H) *in order to face its roots head-on.*

The Five-Card Spread

This spread is also called "the cross." It is made up of one card placed in the center, and four cards placed above, beneath, to the left, and to the right of the central card, forming a cross. The horizontal line is read in much the same manner as a three-card spread with a releasing current to the left, an embracing current to the right, and a current resource at the center. The vertical line is read as indicative of motivations; the higher card speaks to goals and ambitions, while the lower card indicates how those desires manifest in actions, which are not always in alignment.

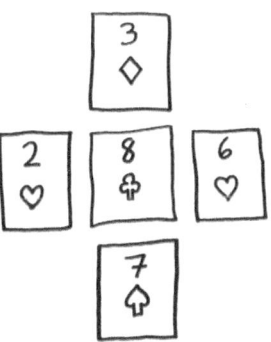

Possible reading: *What you really want is a change in material circumstances* (3 of D). *Be careful of throwing people under the bus to get it* (7 of S). *Old relationships* (2 of H) *can come back to haunt you* (6 of H). *Treat those around you well; circumstances change frequently in life* (8 of C).

Advanced Techniques

It is difficult to talk about the nine-card spread, the sixteen-card spread, and the free-form spread without first exploring some of the more advanced techniques employed in cartomancy. This is due to the fact that more complex spreads use fewer prescriptive meanings based on position and rely more on the reader's ability to discern patterns with certain universal and transferable cartomantic methods.

If we approach the spread as containing layers of patterns, we can choose to mine one pattern or another, depending on what emerges on the table. The following universal methods are especially useful for larger spreads, such as the destiny square and witch's table, but they also allow us to simply place a number of cards on the table without any spread at all and read for basic patterns.

The Color Method

One of the simplest patterns to observe has to do with color. This method is discussed by Dawn Jackson (n.d.), but is distilled from common-sense cartomantic approaches that are very old. Essentially, red is good, and black is bad. If red cards outnumber black cards, the outcome may be interpreted as ultimately fortunate. If black cards outnumber red, the opposite is true. One can also read the progression from black to red or from red to black as indicating transitions in life from challenge and difficulty to joy and fulfillment.

The Accrual Method

If the reader observes the overwhelming presence of any type of card (suit or number), it may be useful to employ this method. Often, there is not just an overwhelming presence of one particular suit, but of particular numbers as well. What forces are "accruing" or gathering around the querent? What do they seem to have in common? Accrual of a particular suit or number can also link cards together; in a flurry of hearts, for example, each number suit present in a heart card may help us to understand why relationships and connections to others are most important at this moment.

The Negative Method

This is a reflection of the accrual method, and it implies a kind of necessary balance in order for a situation to feel "whole." By examining which suit or number cards are *not* present in the spread, we can discern what needs to be restored in order to bring balance. This makes for a particularly strong advisory reading. Tumultuous hearts without any spades at all? The querent may need to harden themselves a bit and stop taking everything personally. Troublesome diamonds, but no clubs in sight? The querent may need to secure powerful allies or work on their reputation as a person to take seriously.

The Ink-Bleed Method

This is one of my personal favorites. In any spread, but particularly those square spreads like the destiny square and witch's table, we find that certain cards stand out immediately. These are usually the face cards, which appear less frequently and stand out pretty naturally for that reason, or cards that seem to capture what is going on very succinctly. Sometimes we are drawn first to a card for no reason we can discern. It just "grabs" us. We can read these cards as influencing those cards touching them just like ink spreads across paper. Let's say the card that draws our attention first, the RDiamonds, is touching the five of clubs; we might discern that what the querent knows or *thinks* he knows about worldly and financial matters is creating professional conflict. He might have more luck collaborating by being less of a know-it-all.

The Line-of-Sight Method

This method is suggested by Elias (2015), though she applies it to tarot cards instead. Essentially, the reader scans a spread to see which human figures are glancing towards what cards. In my own experience, this often reveals a "key" to understanding what motivates the personalities at work in face cards. For example, if the jack of spades is gazing towards the two of hearts, the querent may have learned (or might be learning) some negative patterns from a relationship.

The Nine-Card Spread

Sometimes called the "destiny square," the nine-card spread forms a perfect three-by-three layout. This spread along with the sixteen-card spread are the most complex to read because they rely on the observation of patterns as described in the previous section. Three-card sequences, read either vertically or horizontally, can be interpreted in the manner of three-card spreads, but these lines should be considered together. Because of the symmetry of the square, certain cards "reflect" one another and can be consulted together. For example, the two opposing corners can be considered as a reflective pair.

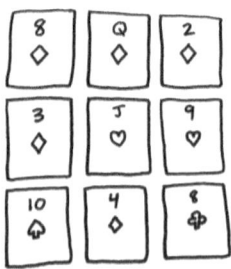

Possible reading (the querent has asked about a new job opportunity): *Your wisdom in using your assets for maximum effect* (Q of D) *is well-suited for this work, as is your willingness to learn and the ease with which you step into new relationships with others* (J of H). *With so much change in the air* (8 of D; 8 of C), *use your knowledge of your strengths when deciding when and how to collaborate* (2 of D; 9 of H). *You're stepping away from a previous situation that brought negativity* (10 of S) *and into a more stable environment* (4 of D) *with opportunities for growth* (3 of D). *Engaging with others in an open way will plant the seeds for some great relationships down the road* (9 of H). *Because our eights are standing in opposite corners, keep in mind that a change in work often comes with a change in power dynamics. The overwhelming presence of diamonds and hearts bodes well for this transition, as long as you keep in mind that kindness to others will bring its own form of reward.*

The Sixteen-Card Spread

This insightful spread, which I call "the witch's table," utilizes a large square of four cards by four cards. Unlike the destiny square, this spread is even-numbered and divisible into halves and quadrants. The two upper quadrants represent that which is known. The two lower quadrants represent that which is unknown. Left quadrants represent the releasing current; right quadrants represent the embracing one. Like the destiny square, patterns should be discerned in reflective pairs (such as two opposing corners).

Possible reading (the querent has asked about some conflict in the family home): *There's a conflation that has yet to come to light, and it lies at the heart of this conflict, between motivations of the heart* (K of H) *and motivations related to work and prestige* (K of C). *These desires prompting action are completely different and need to be sorted out. Acting from a place of love and concern means being willing to let go of what seemed to work before and embracing a new situation* (10 of H; 5 of H). *The near-balance of red and black cards indicates that the*

direction of this situation is sitting on a knife's edge, but your response to the unknown (Joker) *will determine whether your kindness and your energy can carry you through the challenge. The Queen of Hearts, cornered and surrounded by black cards, can read the hearts of others well. She may be able to offer a solution if you can remove the obstacles in her path: a long-standing problem* (4 of S), *an attachment to authority* (4 of C), *and selfish action that wounds others* (7 of S). *The appearance of the Joker in the upper left quadrant indicates that the moment to respond with love to an unusual surprise is almost gone. If there's some unusual surprise in your home, respond to it now with kindness and compassion before it's too late to communicate this. Our mirroring sixes here speak to reaping what we sow in matters of assets and suffering; if there's talk of money or possessions, keep in mind that these things may be tied to an iterative conflict that seems to rise repeatedly. You may think this is behind you, but it is moving towards your family again. Sort out the motivations that are prompting words and actions in your house.*

The Free-Form Spread

Utilizing a particular spread, though useful, is not always necessary. Once the reader has mastered the advanced techniques of pattern discernment, it is completely feasible to read without any spread at all. In this approach, cards are laid not in a line, but in random positions on a table. Their adjacency and positions in relationship with one another help in interpreting patterns.

A Note on Reversals

Some decks of playing cards, and especially reproductions of decks published before the 1900s, include reversible designs, so it is technically possible to choose to interpret reversals in one's readings. I choose not to, and I have my reasoning. It has nothing to do with ability to handle the increased number of interpretations and everything to do with how false binaries affect our approach to cartomancy.

What is the reverse of the King of Hearts? What is the reverse of *you*, reader? There's no such thing, of course. Complete things do not have opposites. Each card encapsulates a world of its own and a complexity of perspectives and motivations. The reversed card and the upright card are one and the same; there are not two, but thousands of landscapes inside a card. One reading might reveal only one facet of a particular card's kaleidoscope of interpretations. Each card is complete in and of itself and needs no opposite. Its positivity or negativity, its "alignment" or "blockage" is revealed by position in the spread, by context, and by the reader's intuition.

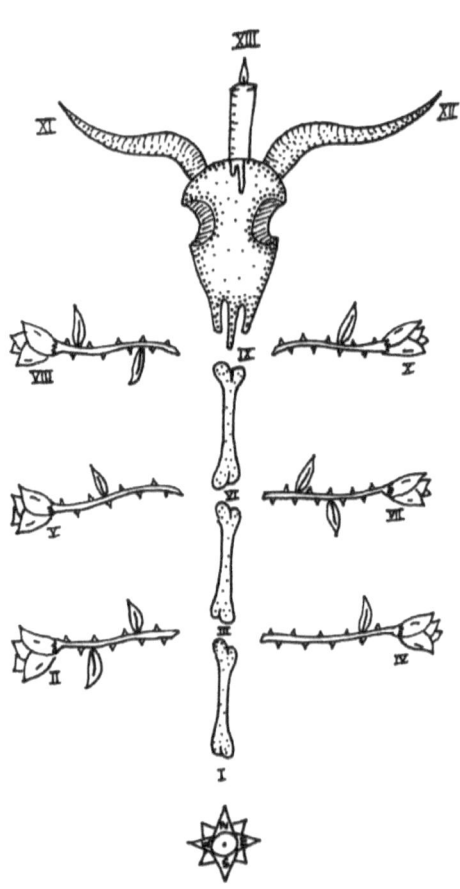

Conjuring the Cards

Although modern cartomancy largely concerns itself with augury, cards have been employed in folk magic for most of their history. Their association with the Devil and witchcraft has given them a dark reputation in folk magic, as in the tale of supposed witches Angela and Isabella Bellochio, who were purported to use them, and in the case of Aradia, the legendary founder of Italian witchcraft, who bestowed cartomancy as a gift upon her followers (Martin, 1989; Leland, 1899). Because playing cards were commonly available tools, this association makes sense. Folk magic grows around what is available, what is useful, and what works best. Its methods are common-sense and decidedly unfussy.

Sympathy, Contagion, and Ekstasis

There are two basic principles at work in most forms of folk magic: sympathy and contagion. By understanding how these two principles operate, the practitioner is free to explore innovative approaches while remaining firmly rooted in the framework of folk magic that served our ancestors so well in ages past.

Our first principle, sympathy, refers to two things bearing a similarity in a ritual act that serves as a connecting thread. Under this principle would fall the well-known witch's poppet and voodoo doll. An object or image represents either the target of the spell, the desired effect, or both. As a cheap and accessible object with human imagery, playing cards work well under this principle. The number cards can be used to represent currents of energy or circumstances while the face cards easily represent persons.

Contagion, our second principle, relies on touch or proximity in order to affect a spell's target. A bit of hair or piece of a fingernail clipping can work wonders when binding an effect to a target. Under this principle also falls the tradition of the enchanted object given to the target or placed on their property in order to continuously release its effects.

In addition to the two principles above, a third principle informs folk magic that involves shamanic or animistic practices: ekstasis. The Greek origin of the word "ecstasy," ekstasis describes a state of being "outside of oneself," and the magical practices described under this heading involve leaving the body in spirit form towards various purposes. It has strangely fallen out of common knowledge that witches were understood, in the early modern period, to attend the sabbat in spirit form by leaving their bodies, which is noted in detail in the *Compendium Maleficarum* by Francesco Maria Guazzo in 1608. This is not dissimilar to the spiritual practitioners of indigenous cultures around the world who perform shamanic rituals of flight and shapeshifting (Wilby, 2003). The final principle of ekstasis allows us to reach beyond ourselves using a variety of magical tools in order to tap into something vaster and mightier than ourselves. As we shall see, the cartomantic arts can help facilitate this work.

Approaching Ritual Work

As a folk witch, ornate ceremony doesn't interest me much. I'm more interested in grounding my practice in lore passed down through folkloric and oral tradition, in everyday charms, and in the innovation of simple magical approaches under the guidance of my familiar spirits. Most folk magic doesn't make heavy use of magic circles, the calling of "corners," or the construction of complex tools, but it is still nice to set the stage and enter the right state of mind before beginning a rite. This shift allows us to focus our intentions and drown out the mundane world in order to make room for the spirit.

One simple act that can serve this purpose is the lighting of a candle. This can symbolize the commencement of a different type of awareness and the awakening of magical consciousness. It is the kindling of the spirit. If the witch has familiar spirits, guides, ancestors, or deities with whom she chooses to work, this is the time to call upon them. The call need not be elegant. *Thee*s and *thou*s mean little to the spirit world. If the witch has no particular spiritual allies with whom she wishes to work at this time, a simple statement like the following might do:

*I light this candle to kindle the fire
of the spirit within.
With this act, I begin the rite.*

Some modern wishes choose to perform austere "cleansings" or "banishings" at the beginning of any ritual in order to clear away "dark" influences. Personally, I find this unnecessary and sometimes even counterintuitive. The spiritual world is not bleached and sanitized. It's messy. What's more, there are many unseen guides and ancestors who may be drawn to our magical acts, and chasing them off with the spiritual equivalent of a blowtorch is a surefire way to burn those bridges. If you wish to perform a gentle cleansing at the beginning of your rites, you can do so simply by symbolically "sweeping" away spiritual debris from your person and your space. You might waft incense with sweeping gestures using the back of your hand, or you might simply blow, wafting your breath around the space and back towards you, allowing the breath to become a cool, cleansing breeze. Some words similar to the following would do the trick here:

I release all things that restrain, limit, and control me. Let them be carried off in the wind.

Alternatively, you can use the following Latin incantation, which is rooted in the Song of Solomon and calls for the cleansing of the self:

*Asperges me, Domine, hyssopo et mundabor.
Lavabis me, et super nivem dealbabor.*

However you decide to open your rites, let your own traditions and intuition be a part of it. I identify as a folk witch, and my practice draws on the witch-lore and folk charms of my Appalachian and Scottish roots. Let who you are be a part of your craft, and your roots will keep you strong. A firmly rooted tree can stand for a long, long time. Research the lore of your heritage and your land, experiment with your own approaches, revise them, tailor them, and keep going. This is the iterative process at the heart of true witchcraft. More guidance on developing one's own repertoire of collected charms and witch-lore can be found in my previous work, *Folk Witchcraft*.

Meditative Tableaus

One of the first magical exercises the cartomancer might approach is the use of the meditative tableau. This is, simply put, a way to arrange cards purposefully in order to focus the mind on a clearly articulated intention. The tableau can be simple or ornate, small or large; its composition is dictated entirely by the needs and preferences of the witch.

To begin, gather at least one card representing the current state of things and the nature of the problem. Next, gather at least one card representing the desired result. In order to connect these two and form a bridge between them, we will also need to select cards representing ways to get from point A to point B. Which cards represent the skills or traits needed to make this journey successfully?

Once all cards have been selected, arrange them on a table in a manner that tells the story clearly. This need not be a square shape; experiment with different arrangements until a suitable one is found. Finally, light a candle and some incense (if desired), and allow the mind to wander while gazing at the cards. Let the cards become like a series of doors. What is moving behind the cards? Open each one, and allow its contents to spill out into the air around you. Call to the powers behind the cards, within their symbols. Feel the heat of the candle. The flame of the candle radiates with the heat of the will. When the power to shape destiny is felt fully, blow out the candle, knowing that its smoke will carry the intention to manifestation.

Naming the Card

A simple rite can be performed by giving a card the name of either a target or a desire, then performing actions upon it. A spoken charm provided in Reginald Scot's *Discoverie of Witchcraft* (1584) for use with poppets can be easily adapted for use with playing cards:

Ailif, casyl, azaze, hit mel meltat.
Card of art, I name you _____.

Giving a card the name of an enemy transforms a face card into a kind of poppet that can be tormented with pins or nails, bound in twine, or covered with sand or salt. Similarly, a named face card can become a poppet used for protective or healing charms by setting the card in a vessel filled with fragrant flowers or herbs, "washing" negative influences off of it, or setting emblems of defense and protection, such as thorned twigs, around the card.

Similarly, naming two cards allows the practitioner to manipulate relationships between persons. This can serve to bind together (by literally tying together with string or twine) or to sever ties if the relationship is abusive or toxic. Note that one of the cards may very well be used to represent the practitioner.

A Simple Blessing

To perform this charm, select a face card to represent the person to receive the blessing, and decide the nature of the blessing to be given. When selecting a card, it helps to consider the qualities of the person. Is this a successful individual? If so, the diamonds or clubs suits may serve well. Is this person warm and kind? In that case, hearts may do.

Let the nature of the working decide the ingredients necessary for the spell. For prosperity and luck in matters of finance, consider using coins, honey, or gold-colored flowers. For health and bodily well-being, apples work nicely. For love, rose petals or other fragrant flowers fit the bill.

Open the rite according to your practice, then place the card on the floor or a working table. After "naming" the card, perhaps using the charm provided in the previous section, begin arranging the ingredients around the card with strong intention. The arrangement of the cartomantic altar is, in itself, a magical act. You may choose to speak these or similar words:

Well may you fare, and well may you stead.
May the waters of heaven nourish you,
and the cup of life, may you drink thereof,
your blood protected from shore to shore
and blessed with this benediction of
[healing/prosperity/luck, etc.]

The charm above is adapted from Scottish witchlore. Research a charm from your own heritage or region, if you wish, and tailor it to suit your needs.

Blow out the working candle, and as its smoke rises, feel the intention rippling out into the world around you. You may wish to sit with this feeling for a time. When you are finished, clear the card of its association with your target by passing your hand over it and willing it to release its ties to the person.

An Effective Curse

Although one probably shouldn't make a habit of it, there is a place and time for cursing. The world is full of people who get away with doing terrible harm to others, and it is an unfortunate truth that often, the only justice a rapist or tormentor will ever face is the justice we design ourselves. As witches, we are uniquely skilled at serving up just desserts. Although some witches believe in something called the "threefold law" and refrain from doing harm through magic, folk and traditional witches hold no such scruples, as evidenced in the great wealth of curses recorded in our lore. (What's more, we must remember that there are circumstances in which even the most devout Wiccan would make an exception and muster up a curse against some cruel and terrible offender, consequences be damned.)

The *Sixth and Seventh Books of Moses* (1880), a popular pair of grimoires in American folk magic dating from the 1700-1800s, identifies the 55th psalm as an incantation associated with strong curses. Together with a bit of sympathetic magic using cards, this incantation makes for a very effective hex.

For this rite, you will need thirteen stones, a face card representing the target, and a working candle. After working through your usual ritual opening, place the card on the floor or table, name it using the method provided previously, and begin to lay stones upon it while reciting this cursing psalm. Most folk witches use elements of religion in their craft, but if this makes you uncomfortable, feel free to use the Latin version or some words of your own.

Psalm 55 (Fragments; Vulgate with English translations)

Praecipita Domine, divide linguas eorum:
quoniam vidi iniquitatem, et contradictionem in
civitate.

*Cast them down, O Lord, and divide their tongues, for I
have seen iniquity and contradiction in the city.*

Veniat mors super illos: et descendant in infernum
viventes: Quoniam nequitiae in habitaculis eorum:
in medio eorum.

*Let death come upon them, and let them descend alive
into Hellfire. For there is wickedness in their dwellings,
in their midst.*

Divis sunt ab ira vultus eius: et appropinquavit cor
illius. Molliti sunt sermones eius super eolum: et
ipsi sunt iacula.

*They are divided by the wrath of his countenance, and
heart has drawn near. His words are smoother than oil,
and they are arrows.*

When you are satisfied, blow out the working candle, again allowing the intention to be carried out on its smoke. Pass your hand over the card, willing it to release its ties to the target before removing the stones.

Cartomantic Sigils

Since a tableau of cards arranged to spell out an intention is itself a sort of composition, it makes sense to consider its translation into the language of symbols. This resulting sigil can be

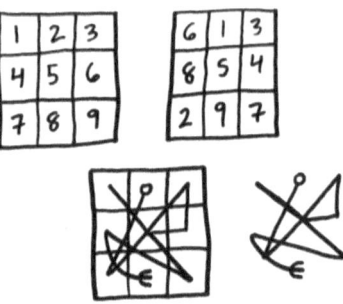

etched onto treasures, drawn on notes of paper to be burned, traced upon the air, drawn in oil or water upon the body, or carved into candles. The clever witch will find many ways of translating a series of cards into a sigil, but one simple method involves the use of nine cards.

First, select and arrange nine cards in a narrative sequence moving from the present situation to the desired outcome. This sequence should tell the story in a clear arc. Next, write down the order of the cards on a slip of paper so that you don't forget their sequence.

The last step in forming the sigil is to shuffle the cards, then place them in a nine-by-nine square in a random order. By following the trajectory of the original sequence in your notes, this square is easily translated into a sigil. For a brief and simple working, trace the sigil onto a piece of paper and burn it while focusing all of your will on the outcome.

Cartomantic Incantatory Formulae

Many incantations passed down to us in grimoires and collections of folklore sound like gibberish. Some of these, especially in the grimoire tradition, feature language adapted from garbled Latin since those in the British Isles found the language of the church strange and magical in nature. Others seem to be the result of codified or garbled words meaningful to the practitioner who recorded them. Still others may be words revealed by spirits conjured by the practitioner and shared via dreams or visions. In cartomancy, we can use intention-derived tableaus in order to generate codified incantations of our very own. These incantations can be chanted in rituals, inscribed on objects, or simply spoken with strong intention as magical acts in their own right.

For this process, we'll need to ascribe letters to cards in a flexible system that allows for play and leaves room for the stylistic preferences of the witch. Since we have a deck of fifty-two cards (not counting any jokers), we can divide the deck into red and black cards in order to arrive at twenty-six letter designations, the number of letters in the English alphabet:

Red Cards (Hearts and Diamonds)

Ace	A
Two	B
Three	C
Four	D
Five	E
Six	F
Seven	G
Eight	H
Nine	I
Ten	J
Jack	K

Queen	L
King	M

Black Cards (Spades and Clubs)

Ace	N
Two	O
Three	P
Four	Q
Five	R
Six	S
Seven	T
Eight	U
Nine	V
Ten	W
Jack	X
Queen	Y
King	Z

Because there are two suits for each color, this allows for the repetition of letters, which is a common linguistic element we should preserve, in a way that other systems might not.

It is recommended that the witch form incantations by first laying out cards around an intention, beginning again with a card representing the current state of things and ending with a card representing the desired outcome. Between these cards should be placed, again, those cards representing the path from the present to the arrival at the intended future. These cards can then be translated into letters using the system above, and the final product will be a unique incantatory creation that sigilizes the intention into a verbal form. Note that, in order to form pronounceable words, it may be necessary to insert additional vowels between adjacent consonants. Play with this process until you arrive at an incantation that works for you.

Magic Squares

The magic square is another type of sigil that can be used for talismans, traced on paper to be burned, and implemented in many other forms of magic rite. It consists of a grid filled with esoteric letters. I have always been fond of the Theban alphabet for this purpose; its use in magic is quite old, though its origins are uncertain, most likely a practitioner-created alphabet based on spirit guidance and channeled letter forms.

To begin, form a square tableau of any size made up of cards that spell out the story of the manifestation desired. As always, it is best to begin with the current circumstance and work your way toward the outcome. These cards are then translated into their Theban letter counterparts for the purposes of constructing the magic square. Theban doesn't contain all the same letters as the English alphabet, so although we can divide the cards again into red and black groupings, some letters will still need to repeat:

Red Cards (Hearts and Diamonds)

Ace	♄	Two	♀
Three	♏	Four	♏
Five	♌	Six	♏
Seven	♓	Eight	♃
Nine	♍	Ten	♍
Jack	♏	Queen	♑
King	♌		

Black Cards (Spades and Clubs)

Ace	♍	Two	♏
Three	♏	Four	♀
Five	♏	Six	♉
Seven	♓	Eight	♈
Nine	♈	Ten	♈♈
Jack	♍♏	Queen	♏
King	♏		

Spirit Conjuration

Witches have long associated with spirits. It is often from the otherworld that we receive our most precious guidance, teachings, and unique magical practices, either via familiar spirits, guides, ancestors, or deities associated with witches past. In cartomancy, we have a tool uniquely positioned to invite, and if necessary, to constrain spirits, while simultaneously supplying them the means to communicate wishes, intentions, and esoteric offerings to the witch.

The following rite, adapted from the playing-card based summoning rite provided in Leland's (1899) *Aradia*, uses cards in two ways: some cards become a table or box within which the spirit is summoned and contained, while others are used to communicate with the spirit directly. First, the witch should gather a number of cards that describe the nature of the spirit to be summoned. Nine, twelve, or sixteen cards are recommended since these numbers can easily form a fitting rectangular shape without sapping too many cards from the deck. (We will need other cards for the other piece of this rite.)

Once they are laid out in a square, candles

should be lit at the four corners, and incense offered in the center of the square of cards in order to attract the spirit. (Place the incense on something ceramic so as not to burn the playing cards underneath.) The witch should then call out to the spirit using this or a similar incantation:

I conjure not these sixteen cards.
I conjure sixteen ancestors, sixteen old ones, sixteen mighty spirits, sixteen beloved powers,
teachers, and guides.
I conjure sixteen spirits superior in might to the spirit
_____.
Let these sixteen bring forth and surround the spirit
_____.
Spirit _____, we call to you.
Spirit _____, be in our presence now.

Once the presence of the spirit is fully felt, it is time to communicate. Use the remaining cards in order to answer specific questions. If this spirit is deemed a trustworthy friend, the cards can be used to derive sigils and incantations to be incorporated into the witch's practice. This ritual's combination of safeguards and open communication can be a way to initiate contact with a possible familiar spirit and open the door to a relationship that may be fruitful for years to come.

If you choose to end the rite at any time, either because the work is finished or because you feel uncomfortable with the spirit's presence, simply call on the sixteen (or nine, or twelve) spirits to end the connection, using these or similar words:

*Sixteen great ones, I ask that you end this rite
and draw closed the door between worlds.*

Because the platform of the conjuring is itself made up of sixteen spirits allied with the witch, there is no need to be afraid. They can, at any time, safely escort the spirit to its home and close the door.

Sending the Devils

In *Gypsy Sorcery and Fortune Telling*, Charles Leland (1891) provides a curious formula collected from his research on witch-lore in Europe. In this charm, the witch conjures twenty-five cards as "devils" in order to carry out her will. Witches uncomfortable with the terminology of "devils" (which is, etymologically speaking, derived from "little god" and has been used to refer to a variety of spirits, both malicious and benign) can clearly substitute the word "spirits" or another of their choosing.

First, gather a number of cards representing the powers needed to accomplish the feat at hand. There need not be twenty-five cards; one can easily use any other number. Once the cards have been selected, open the rite as usual, and begin the incantation:

Ye are twenty-five (or any number) *cards.*
Become ye twenty-five devils.
Enter the air, the earth, and the sky,
into every barrier between me and my desire
in order to _____.

Alternatively, one might use something closer to the version presented by Leland, though it has a more sinister wording intended to manipulate a person:

Ye are twenty-five (or any number) *cards.*
Become ye twenty-five devils.

*Enter into the body, the blood, and the soul,
into the senses and faculties of _____
in order to _____.*

When you sense that the devils have been "sent," blow out the working candle, knowing that your spirits will take care of the rest.

Arrangements for Seasons and Sabbats

Some rites are not intended to produce specific magical effects, but rather, work to better align us with the ebb and flow of the cycles of nature around us and open us up to the current of wisdom that flows from what traditional and folk witches sometimes refer to as "the sabbat," which is really an otherworldly gathering of the spirits of witches and those spirits who teach and guide us in our arts. Cartomancy can provide a kind of makeshift altar for this kind of working, and playing cards can be incorporated into more ornate altars for added effect.

Depending on tradition and region, folk and traditional witches recognize certain "peaks" throughout the year, and although these vary widely, they generally converge around the solstices and what are called the "cross-quarter days" between them. In the British Isles, these festivals are Beltane (May 1st), St. John's Day (June 21st), Lammas (August 2nd), Samhain (October 31st), Yule (December 21st), and Candlemas (February 2nd). In the United States, comparable festivals would be May Day, the "Dog Days" of summer, Threshing Day, Halloween, Christmas, and, uniquely, Groundhog's Day (which is actually descended from Scottish folk traditions surrounding augury based on animal behavior). This is not to suggest that American witches must observe Groundhog's Day or that an Australian witch cannot observe Samhain, but rather, to encourage witches to explore the dates significant to their particular ancestors and the spiritual movements that call to them, regardless of their ethnicity, nationality, or circumstances. More detail about the origins of different festivals observed in folk craft can be found in my previous work, *Folk Witchcraft*. (Note: some modern pagans prefer to work with Wicca's eight-spoked calendar called "The Wheel of the Year," which entails eight festivals rather than six; if this is your preference, I recommend exploring other card combinations in order to derive a system that works for you.) In any case, our focus here is and remains cartomancy. Certain cards can be identified to represent these times, and following a system like this or one of your own design can provide the opportunity to reflect on the associations of certain cards at different points throughout the year.

Because there are twelve face cards in the playing card deck (three cards for each of four suits), dividing these into six units is fairly simple. Because each of the cross-quarter days represents the beginning of a season, the jacks, which indicate learning and growth, are appropriate for these points. Their cleverness in the pursuit of learning also associates them with the one called Witch-father, Man-at-the-crossroads, and Old Scratch. The queens hearken back to the largely female deities associated with these times: Nicneven, dark queen of witches; Brigid, goddess of light; the Corn Mother, who is associated with the harvest; and the Queen of Elphame, which is an early modern term for "elf-home" or "fairy-land." These four will accompany the jacks in their cross-quarter positions.

The kings represent the pivoting powers of light and dark in the year summarized in the mythic variants surrounding the Oak King and Holly King. All four of these kings shall be positioned at the solstice points, each with one red and one black, to represent the points at which the light and dark halves of the year reach their summit and shift direction.

It is worth noting here that the names "Oak King" and Holly King" refer not to specific deities or beings, but rather to a pattern in old world folklore of two kings battling for dominion, each representing one aspect of nature as light or dark, often associated with spring and summer (the light half of the year) or fall and winter (the dark half of the year).

This trope is present quite plainly in two particular strands of lore. The first is the folkloric tradition of Gwyn and Gwythyr, an Arthurian variant in which two warriors are fated to battle for the hand of a maiden until May Eve. This tale has been much dissected by Robert Graves. Gwyn synergizes in multiple strands of lore with the King of Elphame or fairyland, and as such, has been associated with the dark side of nature and the transition from life to death. Gwythyr, on the other hand, is grounded firmly in the world of the living, and pursues the maiden Creiddylad (whose character bears a striking resemblance to Persephone in many ways) in what can be read as a journey into the underworld to rescue her from the dark and otherworldly king.

Another expression of the "Oak and Holly King" trope is present in the legacy of the Puca Geal and Puca Dubh. The Puca is known in Scottish lore as a shapeshifting spirit who appears frequently as a horse or goat, speaking to human witnesses in a deep and booming voice. Old folkloric accounts describe both a black (dubh) and a white (geal) Puca, suggesting an association with two aspects of nature. Storms are frequently associated with the Puca Dubh, while mild weather is associated with the Puca Geal. In some enclaves of folk witchcraft, the Puca is still understood as an aspect of the Old One known as the Witches' Devil.

In my model below, the determination of suit relies on identifying each one with a season: winter with spades (for the harshest time of year), spring with hearts (for a period of promise), summer with clubs (longer days allowing for more work), and fall with diamonds (the time when crops are harvested). At each of these six points, one season is passing, and another is arriving.

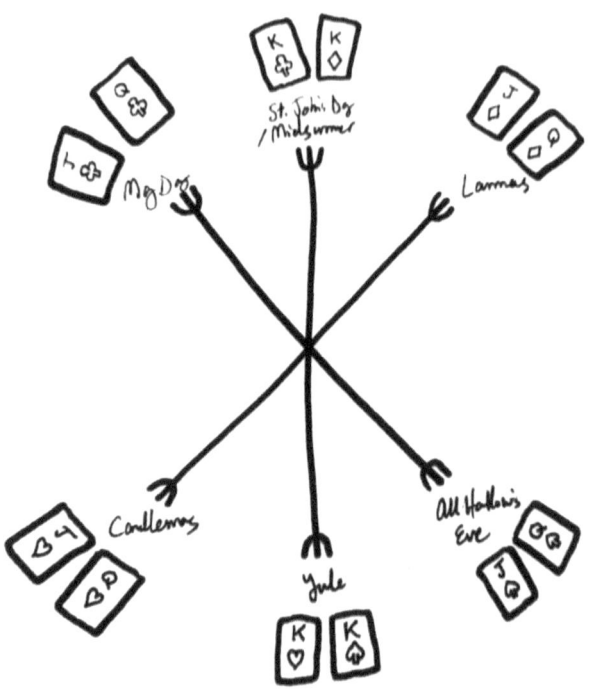

Furthermore, since there are thirteen cards in each suit, we can identify each moon in a year with one of these and select the suit based on the season in which it falls. Thus, if the fifth moon of the year falls in mid-April, the representative card would be the five of hearts. If the eleventh moon of the year falls in early October, our card would be the jack of diamonds.

The pairings identified for each of the six festivals can be placed upon the altar, incorporated into rituals, or simply set upon a table for quiet meditation on these days. A simple ritual can be performed by setting the pair of selected cards on a table before a lit candle, then asking the powers ruling the seasonal tide to share their lessons, craft, and wisdom before laying a spread. One might also ask them to empower a tableau, sigil, or other magic rite.

Conversing with the Dead

It is one of the most long-standing goals of magical practice to facilitate conversation with loved ones who have passed away. Witchcraft's roots in animist belief and practice empower us with the knowledge and skill to reach into the otherworld for this type of communication. However, before approaching this art, which is also called necromancy, it is necessary to offer some caveats.

No one knows what lies beyond the threshold of death. Most of us have our own beliefs on this topic, but to put it plainly, if anyone claims surety about what lies beyond, they are either delusional or lying. Witchcraft and cartomancy are spiritual practices, but they are also common-sense, not fantastical. Let's begin with what we know for certain, then.

How we understand ourselves and each other is largely made up of impressions and memories. Let's use a hypothetical person named Jane as an example. Jane is dead. Jane is remembered by her children as a loving mother. She is remembered by her sister as a wild child and a rebel. Jane is remembered by her husband as a devoted partner. Her colleagues remember her as a creative and gifted art teacher. All of these things make up what we call "Jane," and these memories and impressions do not simply disappear when Jane dies. They live on and continue to touch many lives.

Over time, these memories take on a kind of life of their own. In important decision-making moments of their lives, Jane's children experience sudden memories of her voice and the guidance she would offer. Jane's husband "feels" her presence at the hardest and happiest times of the latter portion of his life. We do not know where Jane's consciousness has gone to or whether these experiences indicate a sentient presence, one conscious of its existence the way Jane was in life. It is entirely possible that Jane's presence after her death is given life by memory and belief. What difference does it make, ultimately, if we are, each of us, defined by our relationships to others, by others' memories of us? Jane is like a cell in a sheet of honeycomb. When the honeybees empty the cell, we can still see the shape of it; its borders are defined by the shapes it touches. In the same way, in death, we are still defined by how we shaped the world around us. The negative space remains, and in its own way, continues to live.

This is why, although we are able to communicate with Jane, we cannot expect the degree of sentience and awareness that the living Jane once possessed. This is also why it is important that necromancy utilize as many rich memory-objects as possible. If we expect to conjure a presence from the negative space left in the wake of a person's passing, we must exalt and honor the shape they left upon the world and call upon a voice from that negative space. Simply hold the memory (or ask a loved one to do so) and call upon the person by name. This may sound simple, but it is not.

In doing so, it is possible to conjure a presence that claims to be Jane, but is not Jane. This is a rare but nasty trick that some spirits like to play. Most spirits have work to do and harbor very little interest in human affairs. The stories of "demonic" entities tormenting humans are the result of Hollywood horror and most people's inclination to view themselves as special or somehow interesting to spirits who, in all reality, couldn't care less about them. Fortunately, in the rare event that an impersonation happens, the trick is easily foiled by asking a question only Jane would be able to answer. Once Jane's identity is verified, cards can be drawn and translated to form letters using the incantatory formula previously provided, or they can be positioned in a spread to help Jane communicate a narrative. In this way, Jane can offer guidance and words of comfort to her loved ones from beyond the gates of death.

If the spirit's answer is not satisfactory and the identity of the spirit cannot be verified, simply gather up and shuffle the cards, and speak these or similar words before blowing out the working candle. This incantation is derived from the *Greek Magical Papyri*, and it is an old and trusted formula for expelling cruel shadows:

Spirit, your invitation is withdrawn.
Because you have impersonated my loved one, _____,
you have offended me, and I abjure you.
Spirit, hear me, see me, and know
that I am neither prey nor victim.
I fear neither darkness nor shadow
for they are my kind teachers, and I keep them well.
I am a servant of our Lady of the Crossroads,
our Lady below the Earth, our Lady of the Torch,
our Lady of the Key, our Lady of the Sandal,
our Lady of the Dead, our Lady Who Keeps the Gate,
in whose great shadow your small darkness
is dissolved into nothing, in whose dread gaze
even the most harrowing creatures
of the abyss do tremble.

Make no mistake; the lady mentioned in the above incantation is none other than Hekate Ereshkigal, an ancient world syncretism of frightening underworld deities, but also a teacher and beloved protector of witches all. Do not expect a flash of lightning or a sudden breeze when calling upon her. While she may choose to make her presence known, it is far more likely that you will simply feel a hush fall over the space, as if a dark blanket were falling upon you. The Lady of the Crossroads is busy, and she has little time for theatrics. If necessary, call upon her in love, but do not call upon her lightly. If you do call upon her aid, consider making an offering of incense lit in her name or of food and drink poured out on the earth in dedication to her.

Entering the Otherworld

The magnum opus of any traditional or folk witch is the ability to leave the body and venture into the spirit world unfettered. This is the true nature of the skill preserved in the popular lore of the witch's "flight." This process is usually undertaken in order to retrieve wisdom or power from the otherworld, and cartomancy can offer a useful door for approaching this key skill.

Not unlike placing coordinates in a GPS, incorporating cards into a spirit flight ritual can help to identify where you wish to go and what you wish to explore. What's more, placing the cards in an arrangement forming a doorway can create a natural focal point for the ritual and facilitate the passage into the otherworld.

To begin, select a number of cards representing a current challenge you are facing or an area in which you are seeking guidance or power. Place the cards on a table or on the floor in the shape of a doorway: a circle, square, or oval shape. Open the ritual as usual, using the rite provided previously, and begin with the following traditional incantation or one of your own design. These words are adapted from an incantation used by Scottish witch Isobel Gowdie, but witches who feel uncomfortable with the phrase "in the Devil's name" should keep in mind that this refers to the Devil of folklore rather than the Devil of Christianity. Still, there's no reason one can't substitute the name of another spirit, guide, or deity.

Through the hidden door I go
to learn of what I do not know,
and I shall go in the Devil's name
until I come home again.

Turn your attention to the air around you. Notice how your breath connects you with the wind. It moves in and through you. Be your breath. Once your attention is truly focused, become the air in your lungs, and leave your body by exhaling. Travel in spirit through the door formed by the cards; you will find that the surface beneath them is now malleable and provides a passageway. What you see and experience when you come out on the other side is knowledge meant for you alone. You may derive guidance, rituals, sigils, words of power, or imagery that can be used in your craft. You may encounter a variety of spirits, and you may very well meet one of your own familiars or guides using this exercise. When you are ready to return, simply make your way back to the doorway and to your body.

To augment their work in this area, some witches may wish to begin constructing their own axis mundi or "world tree" model with cartomantic associations. An example of one such model is provided here:

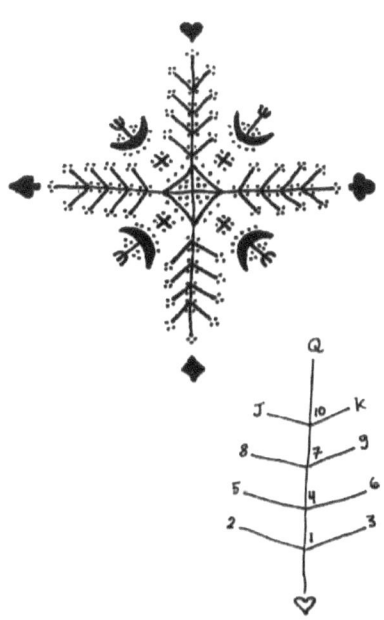

As you can see, the thirteen points on four lines represent the thirteen number cards expressed in four suits. If a witch desired to use such a model, she could erect in her mind a tunnel or hallway connecting each of these forces at work behind the cards, then travel to that particular location in the otherworld.

The use of world tree glyphs to represent relationships between worlds is ancient, far older than the well-known "tree of life" model used in qabalistic magic, as evidenced in ancient Assyrian sacred tree carvings, Scandinavian tales of the world tree known as Yggdrasil, and in the legends and lore of many cultures around the world.

Addendum: Games of Fortuna

"All right!" cried one of the witches that grandfather took to be the chief, because she was the ugliest. "You'l get your cap back, but not till you play Fools with us three times."

What was grandfather to do? Of course, at first he refused, but had to submit at last. Cards were brought, so dirty that they were only fit for a village priest's daughters to tell their fortunes with.

"Look here!" cried the witch again. "If you win even once, you'll get your cap, but if you lose three times, you'll see very little of your cap, or even the world, any more."

-from "Russia's Legendary Lore" in *The Calcutta Review* (187), 1892

Many branches of the witch's card-based are treated with an austere sense of seriousness, even though the tool at hand is at its core a kind of toy designed for amusement. It is easy to forget to maintain a balance between the mirthful and the dire when wielding signs of fate in our art, but to remedy this, we have alternative means at our disposal in the form of games and play and instill in us the essence of the trickster spirit evident in the joker of the playing card deck. Make no mistake, though: this play is still in and of itself sacred, no less sacred than songs and dances preserved in folk traditions around the world, challenging us to mix fate with frivolity, art with amusement, all with the ultimate goal of improving our mastery over these oscillations of symbol.

    The first form of play worth exploring is the use of simple games that draw on cartomantic associations in the course of their completion. Of these, I recommend a game that can be enjoyed with one or two players, the goal of which is balancing or reflecting the currents of influence suggested by cards in order to achieve balance. I call it "The Witch's Mirror." To begin, each player (whether one or two) shuffles the deck and sets it face down on the table, drawing thirteen cards. Players may look at their cards throughout the course of the game. The top card of the deck is then drawn and set face-up upon the table beside the remaining undrawn cards in order to begin the game. If there is one player, they may simply begin at this time. If there are two, it must be decided who will go first. In any given turn, the player will first draw a card, then play a card on top of the card sitting face-up, but the card that is played must in some way balance the current indicated by the previous one. This may require a bit of thinking and sometimes conversation between players in order to draw out the logic operative in the move. For example, if the last face-up card is the five of rods, a player may decide to play on top of it the four of coins, articulating as they do that the slow and steady nature of this four in its suit will surely restore stability to the five of the other suit. Although the goal is to move through all cards until none remain, there is little point in argument between players, since there are no winners or losers, only true balance or a lack thereof.

    Another iteration of this game functions along a similar principle, but is more complex. I call it "Dignities." Instead of beginning with only one card face-up on the table, we begin with four face-up cards arranged in a square. After drawing a card at the beginning of their turn, players may, like in the previous game, lay down any card of their choosing, but this time, it must be "dignified" in some way by the card that came before, meaning it is of a similar nature or that it is bolstered in some way by the other. For example, if the previous card is the nine of rods, we might decide to lay down the Fool, who is utterly bereft of society's obligations, or we might decide to lay down the nine of coins, which transforms the plethora of responsibilities in the card before into a harvest of treasures requiring less responsibility and effort. Any of the four face-up cards may be played upon, giving players more choices as they progress through dignities until the entire deck is played out.

Notice that the focus of both of these games is not on strategizing for a win, but on creative thinking, discernment of currents beneath the cards, and the flexing of intuition as we reason through the many things these signs may signify in different situations. This is, of course, by design. Beneath and behind the amusement of the game, witches are practicing the kind of pattern recognition and syncretic thinking that sharpens us as readers, loosening our minds from categorical thinking and opening us up to viewing familiar cards in a new light via association with others surrounding it.

Although not technically a game, we can also exercise our cartomantic skill through the practice of myth-making or tale-telling, using the cards to indicate the progression of a story with which we are familiar. This works best with well-established myths and folktales. In effect, we create a kind of tableau depicting the events in a fable in order to establish what this sort of story might look like in the language of cartomancy. Here is an example using the old story of Jack O' the Lantern, also known as Stingy Jack:

There once was a man named Jack (Jack of Clubs) who invited the Devil to share with him a drink one night (Two of Hearts). Realizing that he had little money to pay for his drink (Five of Diamonds), Jack dared the Devil to transform himself into a coin (Ace of Diamonds), which he did, unable to resist the dare. Realizing that the Devil was now vulnerable, Jack placed the coin in his wallet with a silver cross (Four of Clubs), trapping the Devil inside, telling him that he would not set him free until he promised never to take his soul to hell (Six of Clubs).

In the course of this tale, several choices were made in order to best describe the events taking place. The cartomancer chooses Jack of Clubs to represent Stingy Jack, perhaps because he is a bit of an adventurer and is willing to get involved in danger in order to learn. The Four of Clubs is chosen to represent the Devil's entrapment, possibly because it is the convergence of power and stillness, suggesting in this context a power trapped behind bars. To represent the deal struck between the two parties, we have the Six of Clubs with its suggestion of exchanges of power and mutually beneficial deal-making between parties. This form of play can be used to increase the flexibility and elasticity of our cartomantic faculties, and to help us frame the signs in the cards as elements in a narrative to be discerned in the more serious act of reading.

Lastly, the cartomancer may wish to learn or create one or more "shuffling songs," which are in truth incantations related to the card-based arts. Our opening mnemonic, "The Devil's Picture-Book," is in fact a song of this very category and can be used as such. The key here is that the rhythm of the song lend itself to the rhythm of the shuffle itself. Because this song has twenty-four lines, we must make a choice in how we shuffle. One method might be to lay out the cards one-by-one, face-down, in a rotating manner, forming four stacks or piles. In order for the numbers to add up, we will lay down four cards, face-down before beginning the song. In the course of reciting each line of the song, we lay down two cards in a rhythm, moving among the four piles in the following manner:

> *Fifty-two (card) the pages count (card)*
> *in the Devil's (card) picture book (card):*
> *thirteen signs (card) within four suits (card)*
> *of blood (card), knife, stone, and crook (card)...*

Because we began with four cards already on the table, the moment that the final card is laid into its pile will also mark the final word of our shuffling song. Though I am very fond of this particular song, witches may explore and utilize any rhymes or folk songs related to their interests and ancestry, and they may even draw from the lore in order to author their own shuffling song, perhaps imbued with unique cartomantic associations arrived at through their own studies and sacred play.

In truth, the impetus to build further upon tradition is not merely a trait of modern eclecticism, for it contains a deep lesson pertinent to the cartomantic arts and to craft of all kinds: that as participants in tradition, we are not confined, but set free by its wisdom. As we progress, incorporating the lore carried on the voices of the old masters, we continue to improvise, adapt, and enrich our craft, adding our unique contributions to its currents like tributaries rushing to join a river, becoming forever a part of its story—a story which is never ended, but continues on and on, a tradition belonging to and made up entirely of us, its folk, who both preserve and innovate upon its legacy.

Bibliography and Further Reading

Ben-Dov, Yoav. (2015). *The Marseille Tarot Revealed: A Complete Guide to Symbolism, Meanings & Methods.* US: Llewellyn.

Betz, Hans Dieter (ed.). (1992). The Greek Magical Papyri in Translation, including the Demotic Spells. US: University of Chicago Press.

Campbell, John Gregorson. *Superstitions of the Highlands and Islands of Scotland.* Scotland: J. MacLehose.

Davis, Hubert J. (1975). *The Silver Bullet.* US: Jonathan David Publishers.

de L'Ancre, Pierre. (1622). *L'incredulité et mescréance du sortilège.* Paris.

Elias, Camelia. (2015). *Marseille Tarot: Towards the Art of Reading.* US: Eyecorner Press.

Guazzo, Francesco Maria. (1608). *Compendium*

Maleficarum. Italy: Apud Haeredes.

Horne, Roger J. (2019). *Folk Witchcraft: A Guide to Lore, Land, and the Familiar Spirit for the Solitary Practitioner*. US: Moon over the Mountain Press.

Huson, Paul. (2004). Mystical Origins of the Tarot: From Ancient Roots to Modern Usage. US: Destiny Books.

Huson, Paul. (1971). *The Devil's Picturebook*. US: G.P. Putnam's Sons.

Hutcheson, Cory Thomas. (2013). 54 Devils: The Art and Folklore of Fortune-Telling with Playing Cards. Createspace.

Jackson, Dawn. (n.d.). For the Witch of Poor Memory. [Personal website, no longer available]

Jackson, Nigel. (2016). *Fortuna's Wheel: Mysteries of the Medieval Tarot*. Renaissance Astrology.

Leland, Charles. (1899). *Aradia: Gospel of the Witches of Italy*. United States: Ballantyne Press.

Leland, Charles. (1891). Gypsy Sorcery and Fortune-telling. US: Charles Scribner's Sons.

Martin, Ruth. (1989). *Witchcraft and the Inquisition in Venice* 1550-1650. US: Blackwell Publications.

Mother Bunch's Golden Fortune-teller. (1857).
	Glasgow, Scotland.
The New Fortune Book or Conjurer's Guide. (1850).
	Scotland.
Scot, Reginald. (1584). *The Discoverie of Witchcraft.*
	England: Richard Cotes.
Sixth and Seventh Books of Moses. (1880). US.
*The Spaewife or Universal Fortune-teller, wherein
	Your Future Welfare May Be Known by
	Physiognomy - Cards - Palmistry - and Coffee
	Grounds, also a Distinct Treatise on Moles.*
	(1827). Scotland: H. Crawford.
Taylor, Edward Samuel. (1865). *The History of
	Playing Cards with Anecdotes of their Use in
	Conjuring, Fortune-telling, and Card-sharping.*
	England: H.M. Camden Hotten,
	Piccadilly.
Thomas, Daniel Lindsey & Lucy Blayney
	Thomas. (1920). *Kentucky Superstitions.* US:
	Princeton University Press.
Van Rensselaer, John King (Mrs.). (1890). The
	Devil's Picture-books: A History of
	Playing Cards. US: Dodd, Mead, &
	Company.
Wilby, Emma. (2010). *The Visions of Isobel Gowdie:
	Magic, Witchcraft, and Dark Shamanism in*

Seventeenth-Century Scotland. UK: Sussex Academic Press.

Wilby, Emma. (2005). *Cunning Folk and Familiar Spirits: Shamanistic Visionary Traditions in Early Modern British Witchcraft and Magic.* UK: Sussex Academic Press.

Roger J. Horne is a writer, folk witch, and modern animist. He is also the author of the *Folk Witchcraft* series. His personal spiritual practice is informed by the magical currents of Scottish cunning craft and Appalachian herb-doctoring. Through his writing, Horne seeks to help other witches rediscover the living tradition of folk craft and connect to their own sacred initiatory threads of lore, land, and familiar spirit. Learn more about him at rogerjhorne.com.

Also by Roger J. Horne:

A Broom at Midnight: Thirteen Gates of Witchcraft by Spirit Flight

Folk Witchcraft: A Guide to Lore, Land, and the Familiar Spirit for the Solitary Practitioner

The Witch's Art of Incantation: Spoken Charms, Spells, and Curses in Folk Witchcraft

www.ingramcontent.com/pod-product-compliance
Lightning Source LLC
Chambersburg PA
CBHW030906080526
44589CB00010B/164